CRUSADER CASTLES

Crusader Castles

ROBIN FEDDEN AND JOHN THOMSON

Khayat's

COLLEGE BOOK COOPERATIVE

32 & 34 Rue Bliss, Beirut

FIRST PUBLISHED MCMLVII
MADE AND PRINTED IN GREAT BRITAIN BY
WILLIAM CLOWES AND SONS, LIMITED
LONDON AND BECCLES

Contents

Acknowledgement

The figures in the text are derived from the following sources: I, *A History of the Crusades* (vol. III) by Stephen Runciman (by kind permission of the author and the Cambridge University Press); III, modification of that in *Survey of Western Palestine* (vol. II), 1882; II, VI, VII, after *Le Crac des Chevaliers* by Paul Deschamps; VIII, after *Monuments de l'Architecture Militaire des Croisés en Syrie et dans l'Ile de Chypre* by E. Rey, 1871, *La Défense du Royaume de Jerusalem* by Paul Deschamps, 1939, and 'Excavations at Pilgrim's Castle' by C. N. Johns (*Quarterly of the Department of Antiquities of Palestine*, vol. III, 1934); IV, V, IX–XIII are from plans made at the actual sites by John Thomson. The map was drawn by John Woodcock, the vignette on the titlepage by B. S. Biro.

The sources of the photographs are: Aerofilms, 18; Department of Antiquities, Cyprus, 29, 30; Institut Française, Beirut, 2, 5, 7, 12, 13; Matson Photo Service, California, 14, 16, 17, 19, 20, 28; John Thomson, 3, 6, 8–10, 21–7; Mrs Charles Wrinch, 1, 4, 11, 15.

The extract on page 63 is taken from *The Damascus Chronicle of the Crusades* by kind permission of the author, H. A. R. Gibb, and the publishers, Luzac & Co., Ltd.

Illustrations

Illustrations

Figures in the Text

Prefaces

In 1950 I published, under the title of *Crusader Castles*, a brief history of the military architecture of the Crusades. The present edition, half as long again, treats of the same subject in greater detail. It corrects certain faults of emphasis in the earlier work, it includes a chapter on the castles of Cyprus, and it deals with the buildings of the Crusaders and their Armenian allies in Cilicia. Little has previously been written of the history and nature of the Cilician castles. Though these castles, as varied as they are imposing, played an important role in the history of the Crusades, they are remote and inaccessible. Mr John Thomson, who is responsible for the sections of this book that relate to Cilicia, spent many months there studying the castles. His descriptions and plans are an original and important contribution to the history of military architecture in the Crusading period.

It is impossible to write of Crusader architecture without acknowledging a heavy debt to the Frenchmen who have done so much in this field, and foremost among them Monsieur Paul Deschamps. In the Appendix further reference is made to the sources which the authors have found most useful.

London, 1957   R. F.

My debts of scholarship are acknowledged in the Appendix. My wider obligations are to those who assisted my work in Cilicia with their enthusiasm and practical help, in particular to the Turkish Department of Antiquities, to the Turkish local authorities, to Mr Seton Lloyd and to Professor A. W. Lawrence. But the blame is not to be imputed to them if a quarrel is found with the assertions or theories in this book, particularly those in Chapter Five.

London, 1957   J.T.

ONE

Introduction

Castles in ruinous profusion dominate the landscape of Palestine, Syria and Cilicia. From the Ile de Graye, where sharks cruise below the castle walls and the skyline is Arabia, to the Taurus mountains, where camels cross into Anatolia stepping fastidiously through the snow, the military works of Crusaders, Arabs, Byzantines, Armenians and Turks, conceived in strife, now stand deserted.

The soil of these bare and dry lands has borne the weight of fortification from early times. The Crusading architects succeeded to the works of Justinian and Haroun er-Raschid. Yet in the long line of castle-builders they were supreme. In bulk and variety their building was astonishing. It seems as though these men in carapace of mail produced in the very business of living, like coral insects, cell on cell of stone. Above the river gorges—Jordan, Litani, Orontes and Ceyhan—their works have weathered. On the plains, ancient tumuli carry Crusading fortresses. Where, as at El Habis Djaldak and Tyron, the rock faces are riddled with caves, the Latin masons improved on nature; the knights lived, like armoured lizards, in crannies and crevices. No curve of the Pirate or Phoenician coasts offered anchorage, but there, too, they built, or perfected, existing fortifications. The fleets of Genoa and of Venice controlled the seas and gained for the Christians the coastal islands which were unhesitatingly transformed into citadels.

The Frankish architects built with a two-hundred-years' frenzy, and they built with genius, taste and cunning, leaving the imprint of twelfth- and thirteenth-century France—for theirs was

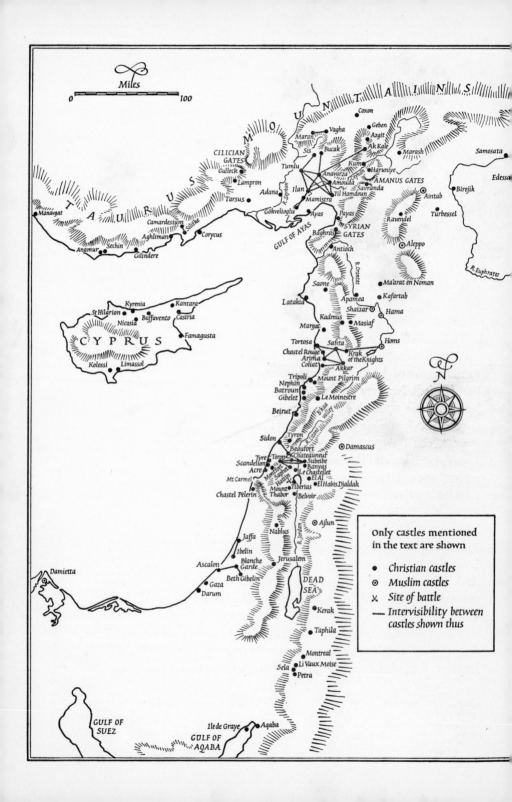

essentially a French venture—strangely and beautifully on the Levant. The mullions and lace stonework in the cloister at Krak of the Knights recall work at Rheims and the Sainte Chapelle; the ruined chapel at Chastel Pèlerin has features reminiscent of the side aisles at Nôtre Dame. But the Frankish achievement was interpenetrated by older, Eastern traditions. On their way to the Holy Land, some of the Franks saw the splendid fortification of Constantinople, while others absorbed the sophistication of Eastern military architecture from the Armenians of Cilicia.

The Crusading castles remain witness to a relentless energy expressed in stone. Above the Springs of Adonis, Le Moinestre, built at six thousand feet, is under snow for several months of the year. It watches a pass leading from the B'kaa valley westward to the coast, so high and inaccessible that it is used only by Bedouin shepherds. At Anavarza the fortifications, a mile in length and enclosing the royal burial vault of the Armenian kingdom, crown a rock ridge looking down upon the triumphal arches and aqueducts of a Roman city. At Li Vaux Moise and Sela, isolated southerly garrisons were established on the broiling rocks of Petra, among leopards and deserted Nabatean temples. At Tortosa on the coast, the Lorrainers built, within the fortifications, a Burgundian cathedral. In the harsh, scraggy landscape behind Latakia, the Normans sliced 170,000 tons from the natural rock to strengthen the defences of Saone. The vast cellars at Margat were constructed to hold a thousand men's provisions for a five-year siege. Whole villages, dusty, throbbing with the cycle of copulation, birth, disease and death, have repeatedly crept for shelter behind the walls that the celibates of the Military Orders planned with cool precision and sited with an eye for strategy.

TWO

The Need for Castles

There were three main reasons why the Crusaders fortified on so lavish a scale and devoted to castle-building so much of their time, skill and energy. The first was the curious shape of the Latin kingdom; the second, lack of manpower; and the third, the needs of feudal administration.

The Latin kingdom which the Crusaders maintained with varying success for nearly two hundred years was of singular shape. The territory, comprising from south to north the Kingdom of Jerusalem, the County of Tripoli, the Principality of Antioch, and (for a bare fifty years) the County of Edessa, was between four and five hundred miles long, but, except in the extreme north, it was dangerously narrow, being rarely more than fifty to seventy miles across. In the County of Tripoli, its wasp-like waist was only twenty-five miles broad. Few fiefs were not exposed to the danger of sudden raids before the feudal army could be gathered. In the geographical circumstances fortification was essential. Castles not only offered a refuge to those living in the immediate neighbourhood, but they provided strong points from which control could be resumed over the surrounding country when the invader had retired. Castles were the key to the land. If the invader wished to conquer territory permanently, the castles had first to be reduced.

On the desert flank of this elongated kingdom the Muslim towns of Aleppo, Hama, Homs and Damascus were menaced but never taken. The Crusaders have been criticized for not doing so, and thus failing to set the confines of their kingdom on the natural frontier of the desert. Though they hoped to obtain these cities, and indeed the Counts of Tripoli were optimistic enough to call their territory 'La Chamele', the medieval Frankish name for Homs, it is plain that the Crusaders did not regard their conquest as strategically necessary to the existence of the Latin states. These Muslim towns at one time or another all paid tribute to the Franks, and under rival Arab dynasties appeared to offer no serious menace, while had they been captured there would no doubt have been difficulty in holding the large Muslim population in subjection. It is significant that the Muslim revival when it came stemmed not from Aleppo and Damascus but from across the Euphrates, for Saladin was a Kurd and gathered his power initially from Mesopotamia. The Crusaders must further have realized that the Syrian desert was not an impenetrable barrier. Water and fodder were to be found there for much of the year, and, as a defensive frontier, it was perhaps no more effective than the Lebanese mountains which already divided Christian territory from these Muslim towns on the desert fringe. Though the failure to capture these towns intensified the need for castles, it cannot be regarded as politically decisive. The extensive corn lands in the County of Edessa were of far greater importance. The County acted as a shield against the main line of the Muslim advance, and its possession by the Franks does much to explain the comparatively peaceful condition of the more southerly parts of the kingdom in the first four decades of Frankish occupation.

Though geographical considerations in the relatively compact Cilician kingdom to the north were altogether different, they were hardly less important. Situated at the north-eastern corner of the Mediterranean, Cilicia is the connecting link between Asia Minor and Syria. It is a link whose effectiveness depends on five mountain passes. The main body of the First Crusade, on its way to Antioch, after crossing the Taurus by an upland route and a northerly pass at Coxon, debouched at Marash upon the bare plains draining eastward to the Euphrates. Baldwin of Boulogne and Tancred preferred more direct routes. Having marched through the Cicilian Gates and down to Tarsus, they quarrelled and fought. Baldwin then marched eastward through the Amanus Gates to rejoin the main army near Marash, while Tancred followed the narrow coastal strip round the head of the Gulf of Issus (Ayas), where Alexander fought Darius, and crossing by the Syrian Gates, known to the Crusaders as the Portella, eventually emerged on the marshy plain a few miles from Antioch. These four passes—the northerly pass by Coxon, the Cilician, Amanus and Syrian Gates—together with a fifth that meets the Mediterranean far to the west at Silifke, are the only routes into Cilicia, and their importance is so evident that the Arabs sometimes called Cilicia the 'Land of the Passes'. According to the inhabitants, the amphitheatre of mountains which surrounds the plain on three sides is elsewhere impassable 'even to birds'. The control of these passes was a primary consideration throughout the whole Crusading period, not only for defence, but also for the sake of revenue. It is not surprising that several of the important Cilician fortifications are associated with the passes.

Shortage of manpower, as much as the shape and disposition of the Frankish states, made castle-building necessary. The Holy Land was lost for lack of men. The army which set out from Nicaea in 1097 was gigantic by the standards of the time. But at Dorylaeum, and to a greater extent in the parching summer transit of Anatolia, losses were immense. Probably fewer than twenty-thousand men laid siege to Antioch. Moreover, as the Crusade approached its goal, commanders one after another peeled off with their military following to carve themselves feudal domains in the new territories. Thus Bohemond of Sicily established himself at Antioch, while Baldwin of Boulogne struck boldly across the Euphrates to dispossess the Armenian ruler of Edessa. By the time the main crusading force reached Jerusalem in 1099 it comprised probably not more than fifteen hundred knights and ten

1 TORTOSA: The nave of the Cathedral. See p. 1

2/3

times as many foot soldiers. After the city had fallen, and the primary objective of the Crusade had been gained, many of the Franks with their followers returned to Europe. The new ruler, Godfrey of Lorraine, was left with about three hundred mounted knights. Although the heavily armoured knight was an effective weapon, and Tancred with only eighty was to capture Tiberias and gain the euphonious title of Prince of Galilee, such restricted numbers could hardly maintain a kingdom.*

The reinforcement from Europe, which alone could have given permanence to the Latin kingdom, was never adequate. Though small parties of Crusaders, usually adventurous younger sons and their retainers, made their way to the Holy Land, serious efforts at full-scale reinforcement met with ill-success. The first large relief expedition, which might so easily have changed the destiny of the Latin kingdom, came to grief in Asia Minor as early as 1101. The loss of Edessa (1144) called forth the Second Crusade in 1148, but even this surge ultimately carried a mere fifteen thousand men into the Holy Land. Moreover the Armenian population of the County of Edessa had provided the best of the Frankish auxiliaries and the loss of this recruiting ground was serious. The disaster of Hattin in 1187, and the resulting capture of Jerusalem, stirred the West to the supreme effort of the Third Crusade. Richard of England, Philip of France, and Frederick Barbarossa each led feudal armies to the Holy Land, but apart from seizing Cyprus they achieved little of permanence and, when they went home, few of their men stayed behind. Richard had laid it down that Palestine could best be defended by capturing Egypt. His successors were probably right to make the attempt, but henceforth the Europeans, who might have colonized the Holy Land, sickened and died in the Nile delta. Failing adequate

---

* It seems that the most powerful force at any time raised in the Latin kingdom was that opposed to Saladin in 1183, and this boasted only 2,600 horse. At Hattin four years later the cavalry was probably rather weaker.

MASIAF: A castle of Byzantine inspiration and moderate strength. See footnote, p. 84.
ALEPPO CASTLE: The Saracen gate and barbican. See p. 52.

reinforcements, there remained only fortification. Stones were made to do the work of soldiers.

The scarcity of Crusading manpower, and the fact that the Franks even within their own territories were a small and foreign minority, affected castle-building in a further fashion. Where the loyalty of the local Muslim population was in doubt, as was often the case, castles offered security not only against invasion across the frontiers, but against revolt and disaffection within them. The Muslim population of Syria and Palestine feared the first Crusaders with good reason, and many fled from their homes rather than submit to Christian rule. There is still a quarter in Damascus called after these refugees. For the most part those who remained in the Crusading states were, after the initial conquest, well treated by contemporary standards. Though they realized this and were on the whole not restive under Frankish domination, at times of crisis they naturally tended to support a Muslim invader. When in 1113 the army of Damascus marched into Palestine an Arab chronicler noted that 'there was not a Muslim left in the land of the Franks' who did not declare for the Saracens. Even the native Christians were not always reliable. In Edessa, feeling against the Frankish rulers at one time grew so hostile that the whole population of the town, composed largely of Armenian Christians, was forcibly evacuated. But generally the Armenians were loyal, and it was a tragedy that the Catholic Church raised difficulties when Thoros II of Cilicia offered to send several thousand Armenian colonists to the depopulated areas of Palestine.

Castles finally were an essential feature of feudal administration. This in the Latin states assumed a complex and highly developed form. Though many of the Frankish barons had their imposing town houses, they needed in addition secure centres from which to administer their fiefs. Such centres, conveniently situated and provided with the varied offices of medieval administration, castles could alone supply. In describing Crusader castles, chroniclers tend to dwell as much upon their vineyards and revenues as upon their fortification. Saphet is praised for the fecundity of its soil and the abundance of its fruits, and mention is made of its two hundred and sixty villages where ten thousand men laboured in the fields. Castles were not only weapons; they were vital centres of business and administration.

Geography, lack of manpower, internal security and administration: these between them go far to account for the number and importance of the Crusaders' castles.

The Period of Expansion

The Christian states passed through two phases, an initial and hopeful period of expansion followed by a long and painful period of retreat. In the first phase both Franks and Armenians built relatively simple castles whose purpose was largely offensive; in the second phase both retired behind fortification of ever-increasing complexity.

Fortification, an empirical art, has few constants. Local circumstances, the site and the problem, are never twice the same. Although the Franks did not think in terms of a comprehensive strategy, the fortifications of the 'period of expansion' may be divided into two easily defined groups. Firstly, there were the castles and fortified towns already in existence, taken over from the Byzantines and Arabs, and often modified in the process. Secondly, there were the new castles planned for offensive purposes. The latter may be sub-divided into two types: the castles near the coast primarily designed to reduce the ports that were still in Muslim hands; and the castles of the eastern frontiers designed to extend Frankish influence and power into new lands and across trade routes. These easterly castles, often remote, and situated many of them in territory across the Jordan, well exemplify the enterprise and optimism of the first Crusading period.

THE LEGACY OF THE PAST

The Franks and Armenians both inherited extensive fortification, a fact that is sometimes overlooked in the discussion of Crusading architecture. They found most of the large towns already well fortified. In the 'period of expansion', they did little more to town fortification than repair the damage caused by weather and siege. The extent of their twelfth-century work at Gibelet (Byblos) was unusual: that little Phoenician port, where the alphabet was invented, was entirely refortified. The Phoenician and Roman defences were replaced by a new curtain wall with square salients, and at one corner a massive keep was raised to dominate the town.

In the County of Edessa, for geographical reasons, the towns were of particular importance as strong points. Their value was proved in the first year of Latin occupation when a fruitless attempt to capture Edessa held up the Caliph's army for several days, causing it to reach Antioch too late to save the city. Had they come three days earlier it is probable that the First Crusade would never have succeeded. Again and again in the following years the defence of these strong points gained time for the gathering of the feudal levies from the rest of the kingdom. Each of these towns was furnished with a powerful citadel, as well as with walls of considerable strength. The fortifications of towns such as Marash, Samosata and Birejik, were an amalgam of Byzantine, Arab and Armenian work. Apart from Antioch, they were probably the best-defended cities in the Levant. Baldwin and his eighty knights found their defences in good order, as were those of Turbessel and Ravendel, the most important castles outside the towns. Consequently new fortifications were rarely necessary. The Latins, however, were kept busy repairing and reconstructing those that already existed, for, almost from the beginning, the County of Edessa was under constant Muslim pressure.

Outside the large towns, the Crusaders also found a number of fortresses ready to their purpose. These were mainly to the north of the Holy Land, a legacy from the ninth- and tenth-century frontier warfare between Byzantium and the Arabs. The string of castles on the upper Orontes, from which the Princes of Antioch menaced Aleppo and Hama—Kafartab, for example, and Apamea, the elephant park of the Seleucid Empire, and Ma'arat en Noman, and Sardone—all dated from that earlier period. So too did Shaizar and the other Muslim castles which opposed the Frankish advance in northern Syria. But as the twelfth century wore on, the Byzantine castles became increasingly patched with Frankish and contemporary Muslim work. Indeed, some of the master-pieces of Crusading architecture were fashioned around smaller castles of earlier date. In certain cases these original castles have been entirely lost. Something remains of the Byzantine castles at Saone and Anavarza, but nothing at Silifke. The original castle on the site of Krak of the Knights has disappeared, and so has that on the site of Margat. Most of this Crusading reconstruction was done in the period of retreat, but Saone (*c.* 1120) and the first Frankish castle at Krak of the Knights (before 1142) were fine examples of early Latin work. More will be said of both these castles in Chapter Eight.

The Armenians inherited a number of the Byzantine castles in good repair. Ak Kale, Azgit and one or two more in the moun-tains were situated in positions so strong that no alterations were deemed necessary. Fortunately they remain intact. Elsewhere, as at Vagha, Gulleck, and Savranda, the Armenians replaced Byzan-tine work. These castles are typical of Armenian fortification in the years of expansion. They are all on precipitous mountain sites, chosen chiefly for their natural strength. It was with reason that the twelfth-century Armenian rulers called themselves Kings of the Mountain. They coveted the rich cities and seaports of the plain, but as often as they captured them they were driven back to seek refuge in the wild rocks of the Taurus, gashed by deep ravines. Here the mountaineers' local knowledge made ambushes and quick retreats easy, and the nature of the ground was such that siege engines were difficult to employ.

The Armenian castles suffered more vicissitudes than their

Frankish equivalents in the period of expansion. Savranda, Vagha and Gulleck changed hands frequently. Byzantine Emperors retook possession of Cilicia three times in twenty years in the middle of the twelfth century. On each occasion the Armenians were forced to give up all their conquests in the plains and even in the strategic passes. Finally they were hunted down in their mountain retreats. When not resisting the invasions that marked the last effort of the Byzantine empire, the Armenians were constantly disputing fortresses with the Turks in the north and with the Frankish Princes of Antioch in the south and east. Sieges and earthquakes, with their constant rebuilding, have left a tangle of styles. At Savranda, where Tancred of Antioch imprisoned his fellow Crusader, Raymond of Toulouse, little remains of the Byzantine fortress except a brick-lined cistern. The walls and gates are Armenian and the keep Frankish. The Armenian work conforms to the sinuosities of the precipitous rock on which the castle is sited. Its defensive strength was enormous, but nature had done so much that there was little for art to add. Similarly at Vagha the rock ridge narrows in the centre of the castle to a path only a few inches wide. Such sites scarcely encouraged the development of any definite style of fortification. Yet these Armenian castles were serious works. Their bossed masonry, especially on the outer faces of walls, was carefully drafted and well bonded. They contained machicolation, bent entrances and concealed posterns; rock-cut cisterns, chapels and store rooms. Armenian building of this period is generally more sophisticated —as in the entrance arrangement at Vagha, for example—if less massive than Frankish work of about the same time.

OFFENSIVE CASTLES (1)

It is a remarkable fact that the first Crusaders marched four hundred-odd miles from Antioch to Jerusalem without taking a single castle or fortified town of major importance. Though victorious in the field, they thus found themselves masters of no more than the immediate neighbourhood of Antioch and of Jerusalem. Their situation illustrates both the limitation and the value of fortification. Castles in themselves cannot prevent an invading army marching where it pleases, but if conquest is to be permanent the castles must eventually be taken. The reduction of the fortified Muslim towns that they had by-passed was the Crusaders' first and logical objective after the fall of Jerusalem. To achieve it they built their earliest castles.

Already in 1097 the Crusaders had constructed small forts to blockade Antioch. Toron in the Galilean hills followed in 1103. Built by Hugh of St Omer, it was intended both to keep the Muslim garrison of Tyre under constant pressure and to prevent raiding sorties. The reduction of Tyre, however, was to prove long and difficult, and in 1116 a second castle to supplement Toron was built south of the city, at Scandelion. Even so, Tyre did not fall until 1124. To reduce Tripoli, Raymond of Toulouse, in much the same way, built a castle outside the walls in 1103. The town fell four years later. Raymond's castle, called Mount Pilgrim, was a large rectangular building with shallow square towers. Partly reconstructed, it still stands overlooking the port.

An even more striking example of the use of 'blockading' castles by the Crusaders was at Ascalon. This Muslim port was a constant menace to the kingdom of Jerusalem. Armies from Egypt assembled there for raids on Palestine, and the garrison harassed the pilgrim road from Jaffa to Jerusalem. Baldwin I (1100–18) consequently built a screen of small forts to defend the road. When these proved ineffective, his successor, Fulk of Anjou (1131–44), grandfather of Henry Plantagenet, erected three large square forts, each with a keep in the middle, to maintain pressure on Ascalon. These—Blanche Garde, Ibelin and Beth Gibelin—

formed a ring which was completed in 1149 by the building of a castle at Gaza. The pressure was successful: Ascalon fell at last in 1153.

OFFENSIVE CASTLES (II)

Castles were also employed offensively in the eastward expansion of the Crusading states. A curious example is the castle of El Habis Djaldak, which consists of a series of caves cut in the side of a cliff and approached only by a goat track. There could hardly be a site more suited for passive defence, yet its purpose was offensive. So long as a Frankish garrison held El Habis Djaldak, it controlled the revenues from good farm land east of the natural frontier of the Jordan. The castle constituted a bold incursion into Muslim territory.

More important, and better illustrative of the value and potentialities of offensive fortification in the 'period of expansion', are Subeibe under Hermon and the castles of the territory which the Franks called 'La Terre oultre le Jourdain'. Subeibe served a double purpose. It lay like a couched dog upon the slopes below Mount Hermon and overlooked the easiest road by which the Muslims of Damascus could raid Tyre and Galilee. In turn, it was itself within striking distance of Damascus. It helped to hold down the local Muslim population and to give security and prosperity to the town of Banyas on the road below it. Its mere existence caused the ruler of Damascus to agree to divide the revenue from a wide area with Renier Brus, lord of Subeibe. The castle was probably built about 1141. After its capture by Nur ed-Din in 1164, perhaps with the help of treachery, it was never recovered by the Franks.

The castles of La Terre oultre le Jourdain resisted for a generation longer. They marked the greatest expansion of Frankish territory after the initial conquest of the kingdom. In 1115

Baldwin I found among the wild Idumaean hills a circular mound divided from its neighbours by a deep natural fosse. There he built Montreal. The present castle, though largely rebuilt by the Saracens, still shows the rugged strength of Baldwin's walls. The construction of its well, one of the deepest in any Crusading castle, was a major feat. Baldwin's venture was a success. By virtue of their base at Montreal, the Franks took possession of the cultivable lands between the desert and the Wadi Araba. The lords of Montreal exacted tribute from the neighbouring tribes and, with even greater profit, from the caravans journeying between Damascus and Egypt or coming out of Arabia by the old spice route along the Wadi Araba. The pilgrim road to Mecca passed close to the east of Montreal and was another source of profit. It was Reynald de Chatillon's ruthless exploitation of these possibilities, together with his foolish attempt to raid the Holy Cities of Mecca and Medina, which brought the wrath of the Muslim world upon the Crusading states and in part led to the disaster of Hattin.

From Montreal Baldwin extended his conquests southward. He established two Crusader forts on the bare hills of Petra and penetrated to Aila on the Gulf of Aqaba, which he also fortified. Thence he sailed to the Ile de Graye and built in haste a rough castle with stone hacked from a subterranean cistern. The last and biggest of the Transjordanian castles was built in 1142, near the end of the period of expansion. In that year, Pagan the Butler went into the Moabite hills and began the castle of Kerak. Its shaggy walls of rough-hewn stone are peculiarly appropriate to the harsh landscape which the castle dominates. Kerak had its own port on the Dead Sea, a few miles to the west, and it could communicate with Jerusalem by fire signal.

The loss of the Transjordanian castles in 1188 following the disaster of Hattin was definitive. But there is still a village in the remote tangle of hills near Kerak called the village of the Franks, and fair hair and ruddy complexions there assort strangely with dark Bedouin faces.

The Muslims well knew the value of offensive castles, such as the Franks built in La Terre oultre le Jourdain. When the ruler of Damascus heard in 1105 that the Crusaders were constructing a castle at El 'Al, east of the Jordan, he set out at once and, catching the builders unaware, destroyed it, lest its completion should mean the loss of a rich part of the Hauran. Later, during the period of Christian retreat, the Muslims learnt to use offensive castles to good effect. The castle built on Mount Thabor by Saladin's brother in 1211 was considered so serious a threat to Crusader territory that it was among the causes of the Fifth Crusade.

FOUR

The Period of Retreat

Though the County of Edessa was lost in 1144, a bare half-century after the Franks reached the Holy Land, the period of retreat was delayed in the south for some forty years. There the tide did not turn until the third or even the fourth generation. In Cilicia the retreat came even later. The Armenian state reached its apogee and began its decline in the reign of Leo II (1186–1219). It was long shielded by the Frankish states from its most formidable opponent and only ceased to flourish when that shield was removed.

The unification of Islam and the erosion of the Frankish states were begun by Zengi and Nur ed-Din, but it was Saladin who struck the fatal blow at Hattin in 1187. This disaster, the result of bad generalship, involved the destruction or capture of the greater part of the Crusading army. The True Cross was taken, and the King of Jerusalem and the Grand Master of the Temple were brought captive to Saladin's tent. Not only was the Crusading army annihilated as a fighting force, but the defences of the kingdom were undermined. Almost every castle garrison had been seriously weakened to swell the ranks of the defeated army. The Lord of Ibelin and Nablus, who hurried to Jerusalem after the battle to take command there, found only two knights, fugitives from Hattin, within the citadel.

In the ensuing reduction of the Crusader castles, the lack of manpower, now much aggravated, played a decisive part. Yet the castles, though denuded of fighting men, did not surrender lightly. Montreal, Kerak and Beaufort sustained epic sieges that were terminated only by famine. Eventually all the fortified towns and castles in the south were lost excepting Tyre, which was saved by the lucky arrival of Conrad of Montferrat with a single ship. In the north, Tripoli, Antioch, the Templar headquarters at Tortosa, and the Hospitaller castles of Margat and Krak of the Knights, alone survived. Finally, though Saladin captured the Templar castle of Baghras, commanding the entrance to the Syrian Gates, his army was too exhausted to advance farther and Cilicia was saved.

After Hattin, the Crusading states led a precarious existence. Richard Cœur de Lion in 1191–2 recovered Jaffa, Acre and Ascalon. In the succeeding years most of the other ports were recovered. Diplomacy, playing upon the mutual fears of rival Muslim rulers, enabled the Franks to return for a short time even to Jerusalem, and led to the recovery of the castles of Beaufort and Saphet. But there was little relaxation of Muslim pressure. It was evident that the need for defensive fortification was greater than ever. A premium was put upon ingenuity. The desperate shortage of manpower encouraged every device by which stones might do the work of men.

STRENGTHENING THE CASTLES

In the restricted lands left to them the Franks built four new castles of importance. The first of these was Chastel Pèlerin, which the Templars raised on a peninsula near Mount Carmel. Its massive fortifications were never taken, but it clearly marked a retreat; its purpose was solely defensive. Montfort, which the Teutonic Knights built as their headquarters in 1227–9, was farther inland, between Tyre and Acre, and served also as a centre of district administration. But its plan, modelled after a Rhineland castle, and quite outside the contemporary development of Crusading fortification, seems to betray the pessimistic and defensive temper of its builders. Its history was unfortunate, and in 1270 such was the devastation suffered in the territory that the Teutonic Knights were forced to borrow land from the Hospitallers to sow their autumn crops.

Margat, which came into the possession of the Hospital in 1186, and Saphet, though new castles, were built on old sites. Margat, with its concentric fortification, became the largest of all the Crusading castles, and it would have been a splendid base for re-conquest, had the Franks possessed sufficient manpower. As it was, they could only with difficulty garrison the castle. Saphet was restored to the Franks by diplomacy in 1240; the Saracens, recognizing that in the hands of the Crusaders it would be a threat to Muslim territory, had previously razed it to the ground. Only through the enthusiasm of a pilgrim, the Bishop of Marseilles, was Saphet rebuilt, and the decision to rebuild, after the Grand Master of the Temple had at first declared that his Order could not afford the cost (more than 110,000 bezants), was regarded as a bold undertaking at the time. It took two and a half years to complete, and, though large enough to accommodate a considerable force, it was specially designed for defence by a small garrison. Its primary purpose was to offer protection against raids from Damascus.

At the same period certain other castles were reconstructed and enlarged. At Beaufort, where a gracefully vaulted apartment was added, a half-hearted attempt was made to remedy the fatal weakness of the fortress: the small plateau adjoining the castle on the south was only divided from it by a shallow moat cut in the rock, and this was insufficient to prevent a determined attack, especially since the plateau remained an admirable site for the mangonels and perrières of the besiegers. The Templars, who bought Beaufort only eight years before it fell in 1268, were aware of the danger and tried to counter it by building an outwork to defend the plateau. But this proved inadequate. In the period of expansion a similar problem had been solved by hewing a rock moat at Saone. Now, however, the Crusaders no longer had the confidence, the energy, and the resources to undertake so vast a work.

Krak of the Knights suffered from a similar weakness. It was from the hill facing the southern front that the final and successful attack was launched. But the fact that Krak withstood all earlier sieges showed that this weakness had been largely overcome. The Order of the Hospital, who acquired the castle in 1142, spared neither money nor energy in the work of reconstruction which made Krak the finest of all the Crusading castles. Reconstruction probably started soon after the period of retreat began and before Hattin. First, a new curtain wall was raised, completely surrounding the original castle at a distance of several yards. Then the walls and square towers of the old castle were largely encased within a gigantic talus and provided with round bastions. A triangular outwork with a rock moat was projected southwards. Even at the end of the period of retreat, when the maze-like entrance arrangement was further elaborated, work continued at Krak. By then, the Grand Master of the Hospital was complaining of Muslim incursions that meant dwindling revenue, and of difficulty in meeting the expenses of the castle. It had become a lonely outpost, no longer able to assure the security of the neighbouring villages. Its garrison had shrunk, too, and Krak was forced to operate entirely on the defensive.

As it grew evident that the Crusaders were never again likely to assume the offensive, grim, last-ditch defence became the keynote of Frankish work. It was in this frame of mind that the strategic bastions of Syria and Cilicia, whose names are first evoked when one speaks of Crusading architecture, were elaborated. Fortunately their remote and forbidding sites have in many cases assured their preservation since the thirteenth and fourteenth centuries when their military life ended. They remain deserted in their strength. All are wrapped in silence, pointed and palpable;

a silence that the bark of a fox or the mewing of a kestrel on the broken parapets merely accentuates. The only real, the only admissible, sounds here are the clank of armour echoing on the bare hills and voices bawling from the watch-towers in medieval French.

THE TOWN DEFENCES

While the celibate Orders kept watch in these lonely bastions, life in the cities of the sea coast became gayer and more frantic. Travellers to the Holy Land spoke with disapproval of the luxurious and thriftless habits which they saw at Acre and Jaffa. None the less, the defences of the sea-ports, which had been adequate only for the period of expansion, were systematically strengthened. Richard refortified Ascalon in 1192 and Jaffa in 1193; the citadel of Tyre was built about 1210; the walls of Beirut, razed after the Third Crusade, were rebuilt by the rich Ibelins; the island castle at Sidon went up in 1228; and a generation later Saint Louis undertook extensive harbour fortifications up and down the coast. In particular, the fortifications of Acre were as massive as the military masons, working almost to the last hour of Crusader occupation, could make them. The plan of their double walls had one remarkable defect and peculiarity. Normally where double walls existed, as at Krak for example, or at Chastel Pèlerin, the towers were spaced so that those of the inner ward did not stand directly behind those of the outer, thus enabling the garrison to subject an attacking force to fire from two lines of towers. At Acre, such provision was rarely made. Another peculiarity at Acre was the situation of the citadel, entirely enclosed within the fortifications as a result of extending the town walls. It was the medieval habit in Palestine, as in Europe, to place the citadel or castle of a town at a corner of the town walls, having direct access to the open country. If the town fell, or rose in

4 CHASTEL ROUGE: See p. 43.

5 SAFITA: The Keep. The modern village has crept within the circuit c
    the castle walls. See p. 43.

revolt, the castle could continue to operate as an effective unit, communicating with, and obtaining help from, the adjacent countryside. The castles at Tortosa and Beirut were examples of such planning. The island castle at Sidon, and that at Tyre which could be isolated by letting the sea into a dyke, secured an analogous independence, for after the towns fell the castles could maintain communication by sea.

The coastal towns have been captured and recaptured many times since the Crusaders left them in the thirteenth century, and little remains of their work. Even at Acre there is scarcely a trace of the double walls and the 'Accursed' tower, which sustained for six weeks the battering of ninety-two engines and the utmost effort of the Muslim armies. The only considerable town fortifications of Crusader date that survive are at Tortosa. There the Templar castle, which had a formidable keep and two lines of defence, stands nobly ruined, and stretches of a third curtain wall that surrounded the town and the cathedral are intact. At Nephin where the Latins made a promontory into an island, there is little more than a jumble of stones; yet this site conveys perhaps better than other, more extensive, fortifications the seriousness of the prolonged Crusader effort. The tiny promontory—you can almost throw a stone across it—runs out at right angles to the shore, from which it is isolated by two dykes carved in the solid rock, the larger a good hundred feet across. The shore falls abruptly away and the island is lapped in fathoms of blue water. This water, of which the galleys of the Italian city states had the freedom, spelt security for a garrison lodged before a rugged Muslim hinterland. The small town which the castle protected was famous for its wines, and the area—typical of the Latin fiefs before the breakdown of Frankish morale in the thirteenth century—enjoyed an administration under the Lords of Nephin more effective and equitable than it had known since Ummayad times. Its twelfth-century church still stands; but the 'island' itself has been deserted,

SIDON: The *Château de Mer*. See p. 33.

BEAUFORT: Its situation above an immense precipice is characteristic of the mountain castles. See p. 30.

probably for centuries. There are now only salt-pans, turf
sprinkled with marine flowers, and lizards basking in the sun.

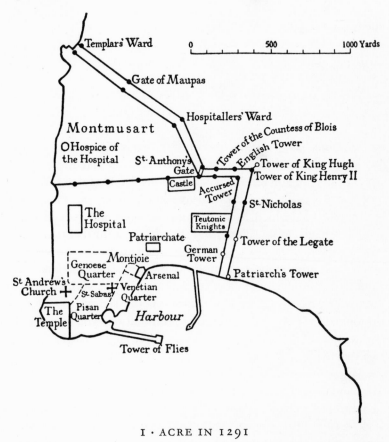

I · ACRE IN 1291

Sometimes the fishermen come there to dry their nets. Their
boats, painted brown or white, bump against rocks that the
Crusader walls once overshadowed. The very silence of the place,
its anonymity, the absence of those tangible remains which indicate the past, yet so often belittle it, make history live at Nephin

with paradoxical vividness. At such a site, the imagination is free, and may achieve a synthesis of the dry historical evidence that has been collected elsewhere. With only rocks and sea for background, Bohemond IV of Antioch, his recalcitrant vassal Renouart of Nephin, and the knights of the Military Orders, stalk 'armed at all points exactly, cap-à-pie' across the narrow turf.

CILICIAN CASTLES

In Cilicia the great age of castle building began soon after Hattin. By that date, the Armenians had captured or purchased Tarsus, Adana and Mamistra, the cities of the plain. Holding the strategic castle of Savranda, they had pushed through the Amanus Gates and taken the remnants of the County of Edessa. In the north they held the Taurus barrier against the Turk, and in the west they had expanded along the sea coast at the expense of the Byzantines. Armenian barons came from as far west as Manavgat in the Gulf of Adalia to be present at Leo II's coronation at Sis. Castles had played an essential part in this general expansion. The Armenians had seized one after another, and used each to put pressure on the next. In this they were enormously helped by the fact that the local population was largely Armenian. At first, when their enemies struck back, the Armenians retired to their mountain strongholds to ride out the storm. But by the end of the twelfth century, they were strong enough to meet and defeat their opponents in pitched battle, and no longer were their rulers regarded as clients either of the Byzantine Emperors or of the Princes of Antioch. When Leo II became ruler in 1186 he held all the strategic passes into Cilicia except the Syrian Gates, and within three years he had seized these from the Princes of Antioch. Paradoxically enough Cilicia was by then in danger. Hattin, though it weakened the Frankish Princes of Antioch and allowed the

Armenians to expand at their expense, in the long run brought them face to face with a united Muslim force which they lacked the strength to resist.

After the victorious campaign of 1189, Saladin's army was too tired to undertake the invasion of Cilicia. It stopped short with the capture of the Templar castle of Baghras at the Antioch end of the Syrian Gates. Next year, hearing of the approach of Frederick Barbarossa with the vanguard of the Third Crusade, the Saracens dismantled Baghras and withdrew. Leo II was quick to seize and refortify it, together with a string of castles on the south and east of the Amanus, which the Armenians held until 1268. The refortification of Baghras precipitated a quarrel with the Templars, and this in turn led Leo to develop close relations with their rivals, the Hospitallers, and with the Teutonic Knights. The latter were granted important fiefs on the eastern frontier. At Haruniye they reconstructed a castle founded by Haroun er-Raschid, and at Amouda they built a castle controlling an important ford across the Ceyhan.

In Armenia the Hospitallers were concentrated on the southern frontier of Cilicia. They held a number of castles, including that known in medieval times as Til Hamdoun, which stands upon a superbly strategic hill where the coastal strip along the Gulf of Issus debouches through a narrow gap on to the Cilician plain. The Hospitallers completely rebuilt Til Hamdoun in the early thirteenth century, no doubt using Armenian masons. The new castle was immensely strong. It had exceptional provision on each side for concentrated fire from archers manning rows of embrasures, both in the outer and in the inner wards, for, as at Krak of the Knights, the outer circle of walls completely surrounds the inner. Indeed, the architect of Til Hamdoun clearly had Krak as his model. The massive round towers of the inner ward rise out of a similar talus, and the entrance to the inner ward, as at Krak, comprises a series of elaborate and baffling defences.

It was no doubt designedly that the Armenians granted the Hospital a fief so close to the castle of Baghras, which their rivals the Templars claimed. When Leo II borrowed money from the Hospital, which he did on a big scale, he gave the Order as security most of the lands on the coastal strip—including cane sugar plantations—between Til and the mountains in which Baghras is situated. The chief Hospitaller stronghold in Cilicia was, however, far to the west at Camardesium, where their new fortress was, once again, architectually related to Krak. Leo gave the castle and the neighbouring town of Silifke to the Order in exchange for the assistance which they lent against a Turkish invasion.

The fortresses lining the chief route through the Taurus mountains in the north of the kingdom were kept mainly in royal hands. Geben, in particular, at some 6,000 feet above sea-level, where the route zig-zags through a defile, was usually reserved for one of the king's brothers. It was the last Armenian castle to fall to the Mameluks, and only capitulated after an eight-month siege in 1375. It was originally a Byzantine foundation but the Armenians added important works. The same is true at Anavarza, on the summit of a stupendous rock rising sheer out of the marshy plain, and at rocky Gökvelioglu, in one of the last loops of the Ceyhan before it runs to the sea.

Leo II's greatest fortifications were on three more such rock-ridges. Sis, his capital, is on one of the most southerly spurs of the Taurus. Tumlu is clamped like a saddle to another of the distinctive ridges rising out of the plain, and the castle of Ilan surmounts a third, with its three wards rising one above another. Together with Anavarza and Gökvelioglu, they form a screen from the Taurus mountains to the sea, each with its dependent lands about it.

The most powerful of the hereditary fiefs in Cilicia was Lampron. This castle was the home of Leo's mother, a daughter of the

Hethoumien dynasty which eventually acquired the chief power in
Cilicia and then the throne. It lies in the Taurus not far to the
north of Tarsus, and was the centre of a great fief with outlying
castles. There is ample room within it for all the offices of administration as well as for a large refugee population, if need be. The
upper ward occupies the flat summit of a large rock. The lower
ward is a plateau, itself only to be approached by stairs, on two
sides of this precipitous rock. The natural strength of the site is
enhanced by a Byzantine rock moat which cuts off the castle rock
from the rest of the spur, and by excavations which have made the
cliffs sheer. This work has been entirely effective. Although Lampron changed hands several times, there is no record that it was
ever taken by storm. The fine apartments at the western end of the
inner ward above the rock-moat breast the winds as serenely as
on the day of their construction. The frequent Armenian mason's
marks in the well-drafted stones seem to attest the craftsmen's
pride in the vaulted apse and bevelled embrasures.

There must have been much fine building of this sort in the
Cilician monasteries and towns, but scarcely any remains except,
here and there, embodied in some later construction. The famous
double walls of Tarsus, which Leo II in part rebuilt, have gone.
The local inhabitants no longer have any recollection of the castle
at Gilindere, whose hexagonal tower dominated the little port, or
of the fortress at Mamistra, the second city of the kingdom. There
is little enough left of the two castles at Ayas, which in the fourteenth century was the chief outlet on the Mediterranean for the
caravans coming from the far Orient. As at Sidon and at Corycus,
there was at Ayas a land castle protecting the town and a sea
castle upon an island at the entrance to the harbour. Ayas fell to
the Mameluks in 1332. Other Cilician harbours, lying at the foot
of rugged hills that make attack from the landward side difficult,
remained in Christian hands longer than any other part of the
Levant. The Pisans held Aghliman in 1613. It was doubtless they

who reconstructed the lower ward of the castle with embrasures for artillery to command the port. Corycus, which the Lusignans of Cyprus held from 1367 to 1448, when it was finally lost by treachery, is a medley of Byzantine, Armenian and Frankish work. Its island castle was begun by Leo II. Sechin, which is mainly Byzantine and Turkish work, was probably still in Christian hands in the fifteenth century, and so was nearby Anamur, with its moat, three wards and thirty-six towers. It was built by the Lusignans of Cyprus, who inherited the rights and what remained of the lands of the Armenian kingdom.

Throughout the thirteenth and fourteenth centuries, Christian Cilicia shrank. The population was decimated by the Mameluk raids, and all thoughts turned to defence. After one of the early raids, an Armenian chronicler recorded that 'only those who were in forts and castles escaped'. Since there was no army in the fourteenth century capable of meeting the Mameluks and Turks in the open field, the castles were besieged and reduced one by one. The pressure and the waiting became intolerable, until at length the last Christian stronghold was evacuated.

FIVE

Architectural Development

We have accounted for the profusion of castles in Syria, Palestine and Cilicia, and have shown how their distribution arises from the history and circumstances of the Latin and Armenian kingdoms. It remains to consider the castles in relation to the development of military architecture, for this underwent changes during the Crusading centuries no less marked than the concurrent changes in ecclesiastical building. In broad outline, the development was parallel. The early twelfth-century castles were as solid and monumental as a Romanesque church. The pattern and detail were comparatively simple, and it is their mass and simplicity which attract in both castle and church alike. The thirteenth- and fourteenth-century castles are in every way more complicated and sophisticated. If they do not have the lightness and soaring qualities of a Gothic cathedral, their architects well knew how to dispose and balance the vast masses with which they had to deal. The junction of a round tower with a sloping talus and curtain wall can easily be botched, but the skill of the Crusading architects and masons rarely failed to solve such problems effectively and gracefully.

The Crusading castles were the conscious masterpieces of men who had devoted much thought and study to the art of military fortification. It was an honourable study for a knight, and one that derived much of its prestige from the ancient world. There was in fact almost no protective military device employed by the Crusaders which was unknown to the Ancients.* The classical

* The connection between medieval practice and classical example is illustrated by the remark of Geoffrey Plantagenet, son of Fulk, King of

tradition passed to the Byzantines, who amplified it and gave it magnificent expression in the seven hundred military works undertaken by Justinian. There has been much dispute whether the Crusaders learnt initially from Byzantine models or whether, as T. E. Lawrence held, their inspiration came from the West. There is some truth in both these extremes, but each undervalues the Crusaders' ability and achievement. They well knew that castles are not ends in themselves, but the answer to certain strategical and tactical problems. As these problems change, so must fortification. We have already seen how the Crusaders used their castles strategically both for offence and defence. They were equally successful in finding the answer to their tactical problems.

The castles arising in Western Europe in 1096 when the First Crusade set out were a new departure in military architecture. Firstly, they were constructed of stone instead of wood and earth. Secondly, they were usually smaller than the great British and Roman fortifications. Finally they were built to a completely new design which was evolved largely as a consequence of a revolution in the art of warfare. The essential feature of this new design was the Norman keep, either alone or in conjunction with a curtain wall. It was designed for passive defence. There was comparatively little that the defenders of a keep could do to harass their besiegers, but so long as their food held out they could remain in safety until impatience, disease, or a relieving force raised the siege. The siege instruments in the early days of the keep were not sufficiently developed to cause much disquiet to defenders protected by several feet of masonry.

At first sight it may seem strange that the bellicose Normans, of all people, should have been the authors of so passive a

Jerusalem, who in 1151 handed to a monk the copy of Vegetius's work on fortification that he had been reading, with the words: '*Sicut invenis in lectione, ita usque in crastinum videbis exhibere in opere*'.

development in military art. The Norman keep, however, was complementary to the Norman knight.

It is probable that, but for the invention of the heavily armoured knight, bred from boyhood to partnership with his horse and to an exceptional degree of skill with lance and sword, mace and buckler, the Crusading states would never have been won. The charge of heavily armoured knights was a new and terrifying weapon in the East. It was decisive at the crisis of the First Crusade outside the walls of Antioch in 1098, and throughout the whole history of the Crusades it was exceptional for a Muslim force to resist the full weight of a Crusading charge delivered across ground suitable for cavalry. When, in 1104, it was discovered that the mounted knight could be defeated if lured into ambushes or on to unsuitable ground, both the Latin kingdom and the prestige of the Frankish cavalry had been firmly established.

The heavily armoured warrior on a powerful charger was an effective weapon of offence.* But he could not always be in the field. When he drew off his heavy mail he needed a shell into which, tortoise-like, he could withdraw. Consequently the Norman keep was built. Though ill-adapted to house a large garrison, its form was well suited to accommodate the knights—specialists whose equipment was expensive and whose numbers were limited. Further, given the character of feudal society, which frequently created a gulf between the knight with his immediate retainers and

* Armour did not undergo extensive modification during the occupation of the Holy Land. The knights who arrived in the East at the end of the eleventh century wore a simple conical helmet and mail shirt, and they carried a long pointed shield, as shown in the Bayeux tapestry. During the twelfth century the use of mail stockings became more usual, and in the second half of the century the surcoat was adopted by the Crusaders. It protected mail against the rays of the desert sun, and it later served as an identification in battle, when embroidered with the heraldic emblems which came into fashion in the course of the thirteenth century. At the end of the twelfth century the great barrel-shaped helm was introduced, and at the end of the thirteenth century plated knee and elbow pieces came in, though plate-

the generality of the local population, the keep afforded the knight and his followers useful protection against a sudden local attack and was ideal for holding down a restive territory.

The keep, which the Franks brought to Palestine and Syria, is characteristic of the early Crusading castles. The lack of wood suitable for beams and roofing meant that these keeps were seldom as high as those in Europe, but they are none the less impressive.

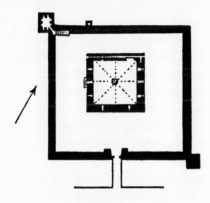

II · CHASTEL ROUGE

There is a fine example at Gibelet and another at Chastel Rouge. There are keeps built into the curtain wall at Saone and Beaufort. At Taphila and Safita, the seemingly indestructible mass of the Crusader keeps still rises above a welter of Arab houses. The

armour proper was a post-Crusader development. At the time of the fall of Acre, the Crusader knight may be envisaged as wearing a quilted under-tunic, mail stockings, and a shirt of mail—these with or without plated knee-caps and elbow pieces—a surcoat, and a great helm offering complete head protection. The long shield of the early Crusaders had at this date been superseded by a small and more wieldy shield of triangular shape. The knight's offensive weapons throughout the period were lance, mace and sword. The Crusaders used a straight sword, barely tapered, with simple cruciform hilt; the blade generally had a hollow groove down the centre. The Crusader chargers were heavy and, for purposes of close fighting, superior to the lighter Arab mounts. They were sometimes armoured.

Crusaders often put their keeps at the most vulnerable point in the castle where their massive defences would have the greatest effect. But sometimes, especially when a castle was situated on level ground and an attack might be anticipated from any quarter, they placed them firmly in the middle of a rectangular fort, as at Chastel Rouge, Belvoir, and the castles round Ascalon—Ibelin, Beth Gibelin and Blanche Garde. This gave the garrison two lines of defence and enabled archers in the keep to direct their fire to any part of the curtain wall. These rectangular castles with their large courtyard were well suited to accommodate a raiding force operating against the Muslim sea-ports. Such castles were analogous to a common Byzantine type, although in the latter the central building was intended more as store house and officers' quarters than as a serious defensive work. There is a Byzantine castle of this type at Sechin on the Cilician coast, where the central building, without arrow slits, has three doors, one flanked by remarkable prow-shaped buttresses.

The keep, however, is scarcely found in the Crusading castles of Cilicia where the Byzantine tradition, continued by the Armenians, is strong. Indeed, the most conspicuous example in Cilicia was built by a Western architect of the Order of the Teutonic Knights. At Amouda he raised a typical keep of four floors, having a cistern in the basement, fed with rainwater from the roof by pipes in the thickness of the wall. Nearby at Kum, there is an isolated keep with a tiny forecourt. Its only door is several feet above the level of a meadow sloping to the muddy Ceyhan. Its simplicity and loneliness in a hidden valley are touching. Perhaps some petty Frankish knight cultivated sugar cane and raised water buffalo here.

In their long march through Asia Minor, the first Crusaders must have realized that Byzantine fortification was divided into two very different types. They were first impressed by the sophistication and effectiveness of the enormous walls and towers they saw at Constantinople, Nicaea and Antioch. These fortifications, sometimes double-banked, with oblique entrances and towers of great strength and projection, were designed for the defence of large and valuable towns. The Byzantine architects wrought with cunning. Necessarily so, for their fortifications were often defended by local levies, who needed all the help the military architects could give them. None the less, the latter were assisted by

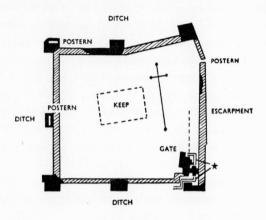

III · BELVOIR

The asterisk shows surviving portions of vaulted passages.

the fact that their enemies, mainly Turks and Arabs, fought a war of movement, and it was long before they became skilled in the science of siege warfare.

As the first Crusaders marched across Asia Minor, they saw Byzantine fortifications of another stamp. These were isolated castles, sited for their strategic position and intended partly as police posts and partly as bases for the Byzantine army. That army was a balanced force of both horse and foot, and above all, by the standards of the time, it was large. These isolated castles had a secondary importance—simply to enable the Byzantine army to fight with fewer losses and greater effect. It is not surprising, therefore, that the Byzantines produced a castle somewhat similar to the camp of the Roman legion. Procopius describes how such a castle should be built. It was to be regular, with a great ditch 56 feet wide preceded by a mound; the towers were to be square, but not necessarily frequent nor with thick walls. In practice the Byzantines had more sense than invariably to follow these directions. They suited the shape of their castles to the configuration of the ground, and employed round as well as square towers. They did not, however, go out of their way to choose impregnable sites, as the Armenians and Crusaders were to do, although they preferred a strategic position, with water if possible, which would be convenient for their armies. When practicable they cut ditches. But they relied principally on manpower. For this reason, and because their opponents were not skilled in siege warfare, their walls and towers were often a mere two feet thick. Consequently the wall-walk had sometimes to be carried on corbelling or arches. The simplicity of their entrance arrangements is characteristic; but they made considerable use of the concealed postern from which to launch a sortie.

Azgit, which the first Crusaders probably passed in their march through the Taurus, was a characteristic Byzantine castle of this type. It follows the contours of a rock which on two sides drops steeply away to a small riverine plateau. The remaining two sides of the rock are hardly, if at all, raised above the level of the surrounding land. The shape of the castle does not conform to an ideal plan. The gate, placed where it is most easily approached, is narrow and has simple machicolation over it, but otherwise is without complication. Messengers or raiding parties might easily escape unseen at night through the two posterns. The towers are not of any very determinate shape or of bold projection, but they tend to be rounded. The biggest contains living quarters, a store and a small cistern. It alone has loopholes and provision for brattices or timber hoardings. The wall-walk, or *chemin de ronde*, was carried on corbelling.

It was convenient for the Franks, and still more for the Armenians, to take over castles such as Azgit, but the former never built a castle on such a plan. To have done so would have been ridiculous. There was a chronic shortage of manpower and con-

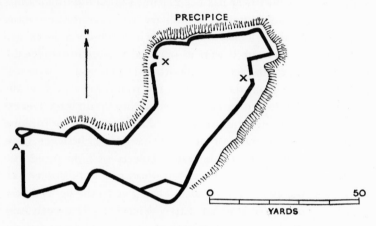

IV ·. AZGIT

A: Main gate. X: Postern gates.

sequently a need for more substantial fortifications. Moreover, by Crusading times, a Muslim army habitually moved with siege weapons and knew how to use them. The Frankish architects were soon building walls of considerable thickness—solid enough to carry a *chemin de ronde*. At their hands the Byzantine ditch received its fullest development, assuming heroic proportions in the great rock-cut channel at Saone, and playing a vital role in castles such as Kerak of Moab, Subeibe, Beaufort and Chastel Pèlerin. From the first, they saw the advantage of the Byzantine plan of towers at fairly regular intervals in the curtain wall. They improved upon it by shortening the intervals and cautiously giving their towers a greater projection. Most of the early Frankish towers were square in the Byzantine fashion, like those which Raymond of Toulouse built in the curtain wall of his castle above Tripoli.

The development of the tower has been the subject of much controversy. The transition from the square tower in the curtain wall to the round tower has been claimed as an important milestone in the development of military architecture, and more emphasis than the evidence warrants has been put upon the alleged Templar use of square towers as opposed to the Hospitaller use of round towers. In fact, the important change in the design of towers was not from the square to the round tower, but in the extent to which towers projected beyond the curtain wall. Towers have a variety of uses, but their *raison d'être* is to provide flanking fire. Whatever method of attack is used, the besieger must approach close to the castle walls. Towers of bold projection enable the defenders to enfilade from advantageous positions with slings, arrows, and other missiles. They give to the besieged the possibility of conducting an active defence and seriously discouraging the besiegers, a matter of some importance for the morale of a garrison.

These considerations were particularly relevant to the situation in which the Crusaders found themselves. Consequently design progressed from towers of small projection at long intervals to boldly projecting towers set comparatively close together. If there is equal salient, there is not much to choose between a round and a square tower. Round towers are less vulnerable to bombardment and mining, and they provide a better field of fire. On the other hand, square towers may have been more convenient for the operation of medieval artillery. It was perhaps for this reason that the Mameluks, when they captured Krak of the Knights, added a great square tower to the most exposed front. Other things being equal, the Crusading architects tended

8   TIL HAMDOUN: A loophole embrasure in the inner ward. See p. ·

9/10

to prefer the round tower in their later and more fully developed castles, such as Krak of the Knights, as against the square tower of their earlier castles such as Saone. But in the thirteenth century, the Templars used vast square towers at Chastel Pèlerin, with gates set in the sides of the towers. This was found to be an effective entrance arrangement. At Anamur, eight of the thirty-six towers are square, and, of these, five are associated with gates.

A few of the early Crusaders saw the magnificent Byzantine wall at Ankara, with its five-sided prow-shaped towers suggesting a fleet of galleys. But the Franks rarely built multi-sided towers. Like many other Byzantine features, they were much favoured by the Arabs and sometimes by the Armenians. Almost the only multi-sided towers built by Crusading architects are at Anamur and Til Hamdoun in Cilicia, where the Armenian influence was strong.

In building their early square towers of slight salient, the Franks may well have been influenced by the similar towers found in many Byzantine castles. When they learnt from experience the value of bold projection, they may have thought of the notable Byzantine town fortifications. Certainly it was not an idea they brought with them from the West. Somewhat curiously, they rarely employed the horseshoe-shaped tower with straight sides and a rounded face which, derived from Byzantium, was the hallmark of the best Armenian work. At Sis, Anavarza, Ilan and a dozen other castles in Cilicia, there are massive horseshoe towers of great projection, seeming to combine the best features of both round and square towers. It is interesting that they also appear at Camardesium and Til Hamdoun, both Hospitaller castles in Cilicia. Their use in some of the huge bastions at Krak of the Knights, also Hospitaller, may be the result of knowledge acquired in Cilicia.

From Byzantine models, the Crusaders developed machicolation, which is first found in a number of domestic buildings near

ILAN: The horseshoe towers of the upper ward. See p. 102.
TIL HAMDOUN: The inner ward from the interior with (*below*) entrances to the undercrofts and (*above*) a line of loophole embrasures. See p. 50.

Antioch, dating from the fourth to the sixth centuries. Its use in the East earlier than in Europe was prompted perhaps by the fact that the timber shortage in Palestine made it impracticable to furnish the parapets of walls and towers with the brattices employed in Europe. For the monumental masonry and the *appareil à bossage* (dressed stonework with a rough raised centre) so characteristic of early Latin work, the Crusaders seem to have gone back to the pre-Byzantine buildings of Syria and Phoenicia, and to have revived the type of stone dressing which they and their native masons must often have seen at the ancient sites scattered throughout the Kingdom. The Crusaders frequently incorporated into the base of their walls the wide talus which the Saracens habitually employed against mining and earthquakes. At Sidon and elsewhere, they used antique columns as headers, to strengthen their walls, a device favoured by the Saracens wherever columns were to be found. The same construction is also to be seen at Corycus in Cilicia.

The Crusading army was always based on the Frankish knight, but as the twelfth century merged into the thirteenth, the archer increased in importance. This encouraged provision for flanking fire and was reflected in the greater number of loopholes with which Frankish castles were furnished. The Byzantines, and after them the Armenians, were sparing of loopholes, and those they provided were generally small, straight slits, on much the same pattern as those in a Norman keep. At first the Crusaders were content with these, and, like the Byzantines and Armenians, did most of their fighting from the top of the curtain wall. But by the thirteenth century, the Franks were building long lines of embrasures near the base of the curtain wall with larger arrow slits and more room for the archer to manœuvre behind them. In both Frankish and Saracen castles these long lines of embrasures, distinctively designed, became a regular feature. They reached their highest development at Til Hamdoun in Cilicia and Krak of the Knights in Syria, where the fire-power directed against an enemy charging up a slope must have been tremendous. The later loopholes were usually bevelled at the foot or had a stirrup base to give the archer a wider field of fire. Loopholes were sometimes also pierced through the battlements (merlons), and the later towers were given a liberal supply.

The Franks abandoned the straight entrance earlier than the Armenians. The latter continued for some time with the Byzantine plan of a simple gate with a straight approach leading directly into the castle. They did, however, take care to put the gate in the lee of a tower where it could be effectively covered. Some of the early Frankish gates were of this plan, but they soon modified it by putting the gate in the side of a tower, thus forcing anyone entering the castle to make two right-angle turns, one immediately outside the gate and below the curtain wall, the other inside the tower. This was a subtlety which had not yet been achieved in Europe. The bent entrance was, however, a device of great antiquity, which the Byzantines had on occasion used, but it was the Crusaders and the Saracens who made it habitual. The Crusaders introduced the portcullis which, though known to the Romans, had not been employed by the Byzantines and Arabs prior to the Crusades. The surprise entrance achieved its fullest development in Cilicia at the Turkish castle of Payas. Having crossed the moat and penetrated the barbican an assailant coming from the bright light of the Levant would be blinded on entering the main gate of the castle, where he would find himself in a large obscure chamber, lighted only from the doorway. Even when he became accustomed to the gloom, the exit from the chamber would be by no means obvious. It is only wide enough for one man, and is concealed behind a fold in the wall.

To bemuse the intruder and defend the castle were not the only purposes of the bent entrance. It was also intended to complicate an attack on the gate itself. The Armenians constructed bent entrances at Sis and Ilan which made it impossible to swing even a short battering ram against the gate. When and if the attempt were made, the whole length of the ram would be vulnerable to fire from the curtain wall above. During the thirteenth century, the Crusading architects elaborated the bent entrance, adding a covered passage within the castle precincts. The most ingenious of these passages was at Krak of the Knights; it contains at least one portcullis and four gates furnished with machicolation and with loopholes from which the garrison could shoot into the passage. The Saracens were also proficient at this device, as Aleppo, Aintab and Ajlun magnificently bear witness. Whatever the type of main entrance, it was almost always supplemented by one or more concealed postern gates, placed so that a party fighting its way back would expose its left or shield side to the enemy.

Not all the Crusading castles, even in the period of retreat, embodied every new feature and defensive subtlety, but all are clearly distinguishable from the simpler castles of the earlier period and, in particular, they exemplify the idea of multiple defence. The concentric castles, with an inner ring of fortifications completely surrounded by a lower outer ring, tended to develop on circular sites that required more or less equal treatment all round. Such treatment would be ridiculous for a peninsula or a rock ridge, where it was evident that danger would be much greater on some sides than on others. But allowing for the nature of different sites, there was, both in the Latin states and in the Armenian kingdom, a steady development towards concentric fortification.

Loyalty and morale were considerations which had a considerable part in planning castles. When the days of the Christian states were clearly numbered, the loyalty of auxiliaries, mercenaries, and even of the local inhabitants, was often suspect with good reason.

It was therefore of some importance to make such provision against treachery as reserving the inner defences for the hard core of loyal defenders. This again encouraged the concentric castle, but it also adversely affected the morale of the auxiliaries. The latter, caught in the outer ward between Muslim foes and Christian friends, occasionally thought it least dangerous to compound with the enemy. Further, if the defenders of the outer ward, whether auxiliaries or knights, knew that they had a place of relatively safe retreat, they were under a strong temptation not to defend to the uttermost the first line of fortification. The Italian military architects of the fifteenth and early sixteenth centuries were to learn this lesson, and it was eventually one of the reasons for the abolition of the concentric castle in Italy. It may have been this consideration which prompted the Teutonic Knights to give Montfort (1227–9), one of the latest castles in the Holy Land, only one line of fortification.

The Crusading castles would have been formidable enough as isolated units. They acquired additional strength in being linked by an elaborate system of communication with neighbouring strongholds. In the use of communication, both by carrier-pigeon and by signalling, it is probable that the Latins were influenced by Eastern practice: the Arabs were expert in the use of the first, the Byzantines relied much on the second. Some of the Latin castles were sited so that intercommunication should be possible over an extraordinarily wide area. From the parapets of Beaufort, the signallers could communicate with Subeibe under the slopes of Hermon, with Toron to the south, and with Sidon nineteen miles away on the coast. From Toron, communication by signal was possible with Chateauneuf and the Jordan valley. A similar network, linking Krak, Safita, Akkar, Arima, Chastel Rouge and Tortosa, existed in the north at the waist of the Kingdom. Farther south, Kerak of Moab, when besieged by Saladin in 1183, is said to have communicated nightly by fire signals across the

Dead Sea with King David's Tower at Jerusalem, fifty miles away.

The communications in Cilicia were equally good. Ilan castle had a visual link with no fewer than five other fortresses. From Anavarza, through a dip in the intervening mountain ridge, Ak Kale, deep in the Taurus, could be seen a score of miles away. A watcher at the east window of the chapel at Maran could see across the pine forests a signal from Vagha. A sentinel at Gulleck castle immediately above the Cilician Gates could observe a caravan two-days' journey to the south.

Despite the immense variety exhibited by the Crusading builders, who made each castle a separate work of art, the general development in the art of fortification is clear enough. The idea of the early castles was to keep the enemy out by sheer weight of stone combined with the natural strength of the site. Generally it was assumed that the siege would be raised after a few weeks by a relieving army. Some provision was made for the garrison to fight back, but the main defences were passive. From the first, however, the Crusading architects saw the advantage of such refinements as machicolation and bent entrances, though they used them sparingly and experimentally. The later castles are not radically different: they are the result of exploiting boldly the lines of development implicit in the early castles. The Crusading architects responded to the acute shortage of manpower and to the increasing efficiency of siege operations with fine inventiveness. The defences were multiplied and arranged so as to give linked support. The evolution of each detail—towers, entrance schemes, loopholes, machicolation—show a steadily advancing complexity and sophistication. There was a double purpose in this. Firstly it provided the garrison with a chance of fighting back effectively, and gave them better protection while doing so. Thus defence became more active than in the early castles. Secondly, the multiplication of defences made the besiegers' task longer and more complicated. The capture of a big concentric castle with its outworks might require three or four separate operations. Such considerations were important in the period of retreat, when garrisons had to depend more upon themselves

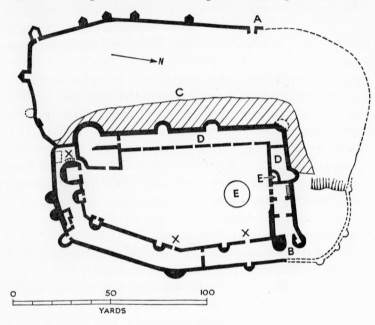

V · TIL HAMDOUN

A: Entrance to óuter ward. (There may have been other entrances, now destroyed.) B: Entrance to inner ward. C: Talus. D: Undercrofts. E: Cisterns. X: Postern gates.

and less upon the possible arrival of a relieving army to raise the siege.

Too little attention has been given to all the Franks learnt from the Arabs and Armenians who, both in their turn, followed and added to the Byzantine tradition. At the time of the First Crusade, the most accomplished military architects in the Levant were

Armenians. Both the military and the ecclesiastical architecture of the old Armenian kingdoms around Mount Ararat show a high degree of ingenuity and skill. The double wall, flanked by towers, which enclosed the capital of Ani, was famous. After the exodus in the eleventh century, which peopled Cilicia with Armenians, many of their skilled compatriots found employment elsewhere in the Levant. On several occasions, Armenians, in the service of the Fatimid Caliphs at Cairo, became viziers. It was one of these who, towards the end of the eleventh century, summoned three Armenian brothers from Edessa to design and build three fortified gates in the city wall of Cairo. This work, completed as the First Crusade was setting out, was as ingenious as anything the Crusaders were to build. Not long after (1111), the Muslim ruler of Ascalon hired Armenian mercenaries, and the Franks were quick to recognize their ability and value. The engineer in charge of the Frankish siege machines at the capture of Tyre in 1124 was an Armenian. Armenian contingents, including cavalry, formed an important part of the armies of the Crusading states of Edessa and Antioch, and there were Armenians in the garrison at Margat in 1118. It seems probable, therefore, that even outside the kingdom of Cilicia, the Franks were exposed to considerable Armenian influences, and that the Armenians played a major role in transmitting the Byzantine tradition. It is safe to say that their knowledge and skill were among the causes which made the military architecture of the Levant the most advanced of its time.

The Latin builders made use of Byzantine, Armenian and Arab precedent; they turned them all to magnificent account. The French genius presided from the laying of the first stone to the finish of the merlons on the parapets. The specifically Western contribution was less in the introduction of particular devices than in the almost loving care and intelligence with which their castles were planned and executed. This care is shown in every detail, in the elaboration of entrances and even in the drafted masonry of walls and towers. The site—or *assiette*, as the French aptly term it—of the Crusaders' castles was chosen with no less thought. Both the general situation and the folds of the immediate landscape play their part in defensive schemes, whose subtlety has, in the succeeding centuries, rarely been equalled.

SIX

Siege Warfare

How, it may well be asked, were such admirable castles ever captured or forced to capitulate? There is no single answer. The fall of the great castles was brought about by a number of factors, two or three of which were commonly present in any given siege. These factors are best examined separately.

LACK OF MANPOWER

The chronic shortage of manpower, to which repeated reference has been made, was without doubt a capital factor in the loss of many castles. At the siege of Saone in 1188, the Muslims found one of the more inaccessible stretches of wall wholly undefended, and the fall at the same date of other strong castles, such as Toron (which held for only seven days), must be attributed mainly to the dangerous depletion of the garrisons to swell the army which was annihilated at Hattin. It must also be recalled that though the limited Crusader garrisons were formidable, their Turcoman auxiliaries, and the local semi-combatant effectives of a castle, were often unreliable. A Turcoman auxiliary had arranged to betray Krak to Nur ed-Din in 1166, but was killed by the Muslim vanguard who were not in the secret. It would also appear that in the last defence of Krak, after a certain juncture, the Knights Hospitallers fought on alone. This was certainly not the only instance when a small Latin garrison was comparably handicapped. Even in Cilicia there was the same danger. At the last siege of Sis in 1375 traitors all but seized the king in his bedchamber.

CASTLE MENTALITY

The great castles engendered a defensive mentality and imposed a psychological strain on the defenders. The latter were always one move behind, always countering, yet rarely initiating, action. The passive vigil, the watching, the waiting, the listening, must have induced, in a man whose lifetime was spent behind battlements, a peculiar nervous instability. Mewed up through long nights and days, defenders must have been subject to panics and irrational fears. Rumours would pass like wind along the curtain: the postern had been treacherously opened; sappers had been heard working beneath the vulnerable corner-tower; the water supply was tainted; disease had broken out; the relieving army had been annihilated. Even the Military Orders with their sense of dedication could hardly be proof against prolonged suggestion. Finally, the atrocities on both sides, the slaughter of troops which had put up a prolonged defence, must have had their effect in making a garrison seize the chance of honourable capitulation. As the years drew on and the ultimate break-up of the Crusading states seemed only a matter of time, castle morale became an ever more serious problem. It perhaps explains such events as the capitulation of Antioch in 1268, after a five-day siege, though heavily fortified and fully garrisoned.

The insidious effect of 'castle-mentality' can be appreciated in the account given by William of Tyre of the second siege of El Habis Djaldak. This grotto-fortress was situated in a limestone cliff and could be approached only from the mountain top by a narrow path that zig-zagged its way down the precipice. It was reputed impregnable, but was captured from the Franks in 1182 owing to the half-hearted defence put up by locally recruited troops who formed the majority of the garrison. Saladin immediately installed a body of picked men, and three months later they were in turn besieged by a Frankish expedition sent to recapture the stronghold. The Franks, seeing no hope of forcing an entrance by the path, encamped on the brow of the cliff and proceeded systematically to dig their way downwards. In three weeks the Saracens capitulated, not, it is stated, because they feared the irruption of the Frankish knights, but because the slow process of being dug out like badgers had broken their nerve. The enforced passivity of their defence, the interminable waiting, became insupportable. Day and night they heard the muffled thud of the picks above, and dreamt of the collapse of the grotto and of every ghastly eventuality. In the comparative safety of their subterranean retreat, they were subject to 'castle-mentality' in its most extreme form.

FAMINE

This, the most horrible of all siege weapons, was rarely of decisive importance in the Crusading wars except in the fateful year 1187–8 after Hattin. Reynaud de Sagette's wily and heroic defence of Beaufort against Saladin (1188–9), perhaps the most famous episode in the history of the Crusader castles, was terminated by famine, as was that other great siege when Belvoir held out for eighteen months. Kerak of Moab resisted until the last horse and dog had been eaten. At Montreal the garrison went blind for lack of salt. Famine also played a decisive part in the reduction of the last Cilician castles.

For a variety of reasons, however, famine was rarely of importance except at these periods and in the early Crusader conquests of the Muslim sea-ports. First, as has been emphasized, castles tended to be under-garrisoned, and there were thus few mouths to feed relative to the storage space available. Secondly there was not always in Palestine that influx of peasants, demanding the protection of the castle walls, that was a complicating feature of sieges in Europe. Though the capitulation of Saphet in

1266 (after a three-weeks' siege) no doubt had something to do with the two thousand refugees in the castle, the local inhabitants were often Muslims and could view the approach of a besieging army without panic. Again, castles were rarely reduced by famine because full provision was made for just this eventuality and the besiegers were often as likely to go short of food as the besieged. It was for this reason that the Muslim army abandoned the siege of Edessa in 1110. The major castles contained vast subterranean storage depots. Margat was habitually stocked for a five-year siege; Krak of the Knights had its windmill on the battlements for grinding corn, and the size of its granaries, bakeries, oil-presses and oil-storage jars still amazes; at Saone the larger of two subterranean water tanks, that looks with its wide-spanned barrel vault like the nave of a Romanesque church, is 117 feet long and 52 feet high.

SIEGE WEAPONS

When the Latins first reached the East, siege tactics were not highly developed, but in the succeeding centuries of siege and counter-siege the methods already well-known to the Byzantines were developed and improved. The Saracens in particular became adept at every trick which might hasten the fall of a castle. The besieger had two plain alternatives—assault or battery. He could scale the walls or breach them.

The scaling ladder was the simplest method of direct assault, but, given a castle adequately garrisoned, it was also the most costly and easily repulsed. Only when the attacking force enjoyed numerical superiority and could afford heavy losses in a number of simultaneous assaults was there serious hope of success. It is relevant in this context to recall that the Saracens could often bring thousands to an assault, where the defenders could oppose perhaps no more than a few score knights and a complement of retainers.

A more effective method of direct assault was by means of tall wooden towers. These, built to over-top the castle parapet (so that the attackers could sweep the wall-walk) were moved up on wheels, and were provided with a drawbridge. When sufficiently close, the latter was lowered on to the battlements. The Franks in particular specialized in the use of towers, and it was by means of a tower that they first captured Jerusalem. The essential thing about a besieging tower was that it should be higher than the curtain wall and the neighbouring bastions. At the siege of Tyre in 1111, one of the Frankish towers was about 65 feet and another 80 feet high. They were gigantic structures which it took weeks to build, for they had to be solid enough to withstand the stones hurled against them by the siege engines of the castle as they were laboriously pushed up to the walls. Before they could approach, the ground had to be levelled and the moats filled in (at Tyre there were three moats). Finally they had to be draped with branches of vines, mats, and damp ox-hides, as a protection against missiles and Greek fire, and men with supplies of water and vinegar were stationed on them to prevent fires.

Such were the main types of direct assault. The common methods of effecting a breach in the walls, an altogether different matter, were three in number; the ram, the bore and the mine. The ram was usually a giant tree, the largest that the district could afford. It might be a hundred feet long, tipped with an iron head weighing twenty pounds. Slung on a frame between stout uprights or in the base of a wooden tower, it was wheeled up to the castle, and a team of men, who might be as many as sixty, under cover of a protective penthouse, proceeded rhythmically to swing the great beam against the point in the wall selected for breaching. There was no masonry that could stand up to this treatment indefinitely, and if the shuddering blows were allowed to pile up hour after hour, the mortar loosened and the stoutest wall in time gave way. It was rare, however, that the ram could be used under such ideal conditions. The beleaguered garrison would lower mattresses or baulks of timber, as did the Muslims at the siege of Jerusalem in 1099, to take up the shock, or would catch and pin the ram as it delivered its blow. At the siege of Tyre in 1111 a Muslim seaman from Tripoli invented grappling irons which caught the ram and pulled it sideways so that it nearly over-turned the wooden tower in which it was slung.

The bore differed from the ram in that it attempted to dis-integrate the wall by gnawing its way through, rather than by shock. The Romans had known it, aptly enough, under the name of *musculus*, or mouse. It was more easily manageable than the ram, but less effective. In 1132, however, the Damascenes breached the walls of Banyas by means of a bore. Working under the protection of heavy covering fire from bowmen, a special corps of sappers fixed shields against a section of the wall. Under the protection of these their bore eventually pierced the wall.

There remained the mine. This was the most dangerous of all the contemporary siege weapons, and in its use the sappers of the East attained great proficiency—the sappers of Aleppo (whom Richard I employed at the siege of Darum) and those of Khurasan being especially famed for their skill. The manner in which these mines were laid, in an age before gunpowder, was ingenious. This Arab description of the fall of Edessa in 1144 well describes the process:

'The men of Khurasan and of Aleppo who were familiar with the technique of sapping, and bold in carrying it out, set to work and made saps at a number of places which they selected as suit-able for their operations. They continued thus to push on with their sapping and to dig through the belly of the earth until they reached below the foundations of the bastions of the wall. They then shored these up with stout timbers and special appliances, and when they had made an end of that, nothing remained but to set fire to them. They asked 'Imad ed-Din Atabek for instructions on this matter, and, after he had entered the sap and seen in person what had been done and expressed his admiration, he gave them their orders. When fire was applied to the shoring, it caught the timbers and destroyed them, and immediately the wall fell down. The Muslims forced their way into the city, after a great number on both sides had been killed over the ruins; so many of the Franks and Armenians were killed and wounded that they were compelled to abandon the town, and the Muslims took possession of it by the sword in the early forenoon of Saturday, 26 Latter Jumada (December 23, 1144). The troops set to pillaging, slaying, capturing, ravishing, and looting, and their hands were filled with such quantities of money, furnishings, animals, booty, and captives as rejoiced their spirits and gladdened their hearts.'

It was by means of a mine that the outer defences of Krak of the Knights were penetrated, and Saladin in 1179, only a year after its construction, successfully mined and then razed the castle of Le Chastellet, set to guard Jacob's Ford on the upper Jordan. A counter mine was, of course, possible. If suspicious activity was seen, or sounds suggesting mining were heard, the garrison might begin a tunnel within the castle, burrow under the walls, and aim to irrupt into the mine. This was a difficult and skilled operation which was not often employed, partly because mining so frequently took the defenders by surprise. The only sure defence against mining was to build on solid rock.

Possibly the most dramatic use of the mine in the Crusading sieges occurred at Margat. After lengthy preparation, the Sultan Kalaoun invested the fortress in 1285, but the engines he brought up against it were at once destroyed by the garrison. The Muslims thereupon set out to mine the defences, and successfully brought down the outworks. An attack was then launched on the main

11 MARGAT: The eastern strongwork, with the great tower mined by the Sultan Kalaoun. See p. 65.

12/13

stronghold, but was decisively repulsed. Mining operations were accordingly resumed and, after eight days below ground, the sappers reached and completely undermined the foundations of the circular tower-keep. The Sultan was anxious not to destroy this remarkable defensive work, the bastion of the castle, perhaps comparable in size and strength only to the round tower at Saphet, of which no trace remains, and to the thirteenth-century keep at Coucy in France. He therefore invited the Hospitallers to send out a deputation to view the extent of the Saracen mine. They did so, and at once realized that further resistance was useless. The castle capitulated and the knights retired under safe conduct to Acre, each taking with him his baggage and a large sum of gold. Contemporary Arab historians, grudging honour to their own technicians, attributed the fall of this seemingly impregnable castle to the intervention of angels.

It remains to say something of what may legitimately be called the artillery of the Crusader period, which was of course available to besiegers and defenders alike. The mangon, which, as we shall see, Saladin used at Saone, was in essence a huge sling. It was very powerful and could hurl immense rocks, but, having a high trajectory, was difficult to aim with precision and of doubtful value for the bombardment of a specific point in the curtain. The Latins found this weapon in general employ among the Saracens, and themselves adopted it in the first half of the twelfth century. That they became proficient in its use is attested by the fact that when besieging Shaizar, a Muslim castle on the Orontes, a single millstone tossed by one of their mangons razed a complete building.

But it was the Byzantines who were most competent in the use of artillery. At the siege of Anavarza in Cilicia, they brought up a formidable battery. Even so it took thirty-seven days to reduce the castle. At one moment the artillery used by the defending Armenian force was destroying so many of the Byzantine

MARGAT: Aerial view showing both the concentric fortification and the vast size of the castle enclosure. See p. 30.

SAONE: Aerial view from the west. See p. 79.

mangons that they were in despair, until the Emperor's son struck upon the expedient of covering them with a thick layer of mud.

The balista, a more accurate weapon, was really no more than a gigantic crossbow which shot iron bolts, 'feathered' with wood, and four times the thickness of the ordinary arrow. Mail was no proof against these missiles, and their powers of penetration may be gauged by the fact that at the siege of Paris in the ninth century a single happy shaft transfixed several Danes who happened to be in alignment. The Franks were expert in the use of the balista, and Saladin's failure to take Tortosa in 1188 is attributed to the effectiveness of a number of these weapons mounted on the keep. At some of the later castles, Krak for example, there were embrasures specially designed for the balista; and the walls at the Armenian capital of Sis were furnished with a number of these weapons.

The third type of 'artillery' employed in the Holy Land, the trebuchet, came into common use only after the First Crusade. Like the mangon, it was designed for hurling heavy bodies, but it worked by counterpoise. A long pole was laid in see-saw fashion across an upright, and its shorter, butt end, was heavily weighted. Its longer end, to which a missile was attached, was drawn back to the ground. When this end was released, the action of the counterpoise discharged the missile. Though the trajectory of the trebuchet was not unlike that of the mangon, the weapon had a big advantage, since, by adjusting the position of the weights on the pole relative to the pivotal point, far greater accuracy could be obtained. At the siege of Acre in 1189, the Franks built an enormous machine appropriately nicknamed '*Malvoisine*', whose steady battering brought down part of the city walls. It was with the trebuchet that the Saracens usually hurled Greek fire, whose value they had learned from the Byzantines, and whose effects were so destructive on the wooden engines of the time.

SEVEN

Castle Life

The Crusading castles with their ample stabling, their dovecots, their mills, and their vast subterranean storage chambers, were naturally someone's property and responsibility. It will be well at this point to consider who owned them. The leaders of the First Crusade brought with them a clear idea of how society should be ordered. They imprinted the stamp of an ideal feudal pattern upon the Levant more completely and clearly than it existed in Europe, where it had developed piecemeal. The castle was a natural feature of this society, the administrative centre of a fief and a focus of power which ensured dominance over the neighbourhood.

Because of the small number of Frankish knights the feudal links in the Levant were more simple than in Europe. Castles and lands were held either directly from the King, or at one remove, from a great lord. The pattern, however, was not quite consistent. In the north the Princes of Antioch and the Counts of Edessa kept most of the lands and castles in their own hands, appointing chatelains or deputies to act for them, and they tended to entrust the administration of great fiefs to their relatives. Thus the Counts of Edessa appointed their Armenian relations by marriage, while the Princes of Antioch favoured their Norman kinsmen. The large fief of the Mazoirs with its centre at the castle of Margat was an exception. This family came from the Midi and prospered. They were almost the last family to sell out to the Military Orders, the Hospitallers buying Margat only in the year before Hattin. In the southern states of Tripoli and Jerusalem more land was in the hands of the barons, who were consequently of greater importance than in the north. The Counts of Tripoli were hard put to it to control their vassals at Nephin, and the King of Jerusalem, holding little more than Jerusalem and Acre, governed a lesser territory than his vassal, the lord of La Terre oultre le Jourdain. The other three chief barons of the Kingdom of Jerusalem, the Prince of Galilee and the Lords of Sidon and of Jaffa-Ascalon were individually as rich as the King. Each owed the service of a hundred knights and, together with the sixty knights owed by the Lord of La Terre oultre le Jourdain, these amounted to more than half the force upon which the King might call. Not all these knights had their own lands. Many lived as clients in the greater lords' castles and many depended on annuities secured upon the revenues of the towns. The rest of the effective army was composed of 'serjeants' whose service was owed by the towns and by the ecclesiastical authorities. Tyre owed a hundred, the Chapter of the Holy Sepulchre five hundred, and the monks of the Mount of Olives fifty.

The kingdom of Cilicia was ordered upon a system more like that of Antioch than that of Jerusalem. When Thoros II of Cilicia made the pilgrimage to Jerusalem in 1166 he was amazed to find that the Latin King himself held only three castles. By contrast, Leo II of Cilicia is reputed to have been lord of seventy-two castles, of which forty-nine are said to have been of the first order. Nevertheless, the Armenian barons were a group to be reckoned with. When Leo III learnt that there was serious discontent amongst them he promptly checked it by resuming control of some of the more important castles which he and his predecessors had granted to vassals. The Armenian nobility, and particularly the royal family, had close connections with the leading Frankish families. Baldwin I, the first king of Jerusalem, married an Armenian princess and set a precedent which was widely followed. On more than one occasion it seemed that a marriage alliance might unite the Kingdom of Cilicia and the Principality of Antioch had not death and war intervened.

The castles were intimately connected with the business of feudal government, and the difficulties which government faced were mirrored in the changing ownership of the castles. The sires d'Embriac, the descendants of a Genoese Admiral, were exceptional in holding the lordship of Gibelet through eight unbroken generations. Few castles remained in one family for three generations, either in Cilicia or in the Latin states. Life was full of hazards and sudden accidents. Infant mortality, particularly among boys, was high. Some families were exterminated in battle. Others were ruined by the payment of enormous ransoms and the charge of maintaining their castles and men at arms. Families that flourished in royal favour increased their lands at the expense of dissidents. Minors and women could not be left in control of the military resources upon which the Christian states depended, so guardians were appointed or widows remarried. Finally, eminent newcomers from the West were induced by grants of land to settle in Palestine and help defend the country.

The career of Reynald de Chatillon gives a glimpse of the diverse currents which carried castles from one lord to another. Reynald, a younger son who came to the Holy Land with the Second Crusade, first acquired a small fief in the Principality of Antioch. He was next fortunate enough to marry the widowed Princess of Antioch, who was expected to give herself and her castles to some new lord. However, Reynald de Chatillon did not control the Principality for long, as he was captured by the Saracens and imprisoned in Aleppo for several years. When finally released from captivity, he found the Principality in other hands. Obliged to look elsewhere for lands and castles, he acquired them in the south, by marriage to the heiress of Oultrejourdain, whose previous husband had been the victim of a feudal quarrel. Such changes in territorial ownership were frequent.

As the twelfth century progressed and the Latin Kingdom was exposed to increasing Muslim pressure from the East, the burden and expense of manning and maintaining the castles (which were at the same time being enlarged) became more than most feudal lords could support. One after another they sold or gave away their castles, until at last it was very much the exception to find a large castle in feudal ownership. The construction of a new castle at Beirut in the thirteenth century at the sole charge of one family was still more exceptional. It was only possible because the Ibelins of Beirut were also lords of the largest fief in Cyprus.

Providentially, by the middle of the twelfth century, the Crusading venture had brought to a high degree of perfection two kindred organizations well adapted to sustain the burden of maintaining the great castles. These were the Military Orders of the Hospital and of the Temple. At the end of the century they were joined by the Order of the Teutonic Knights. As the feudal lords relinquished their castles, the Military Orders took over. In time the main responsibility for the defence of the Kingdom devolved upon them. From the time of Hattin (1187), when 230 knights of the Orders died rather than turn Muslim, to the last defence of Acre, conducted over a century later by the Grand Master of the Temple, most of the heroic exploits of the Crusades are associated with these fraternities of fighting monks.

For the guardianship of the castles, and particularly of the great frontier castles, they had every qualification. From their vast religious endowments all over Europe and their wide holdings in the Levant they derived the requisite wealth; their direct responsibility to the Pope gave them authority and independence; their vows of chastity, poverty and obedience, suited them for the dour life of the frontier; and as undying corporations they ensured continuity of policy and command. The last was particularly important in a country where death was common and minors frequently succeeded to feudal fiefs. These powerful Orders levied their own taxes, possessed their own marine, and through their diplomatic services could speak to the courts of Europe on almost equal terms. Sometimes they even possessed the right to make war and arrange truces independently of the rest of the Kingdom.

The Hospitallers as a religious order antedated the Crusades, and had for long been in charge of the pilgrim traffic to Jerusalem, supplying accommodation and, as their name suggests, looking after the sick. Their military functions developed in the early years of the twelfth century. The Templars, taking their name from the temple enclosure in Jerusalem, were constituted as a military order in 1118. It was in the years immediately subsequent to this date that the power and influence of both Orders began to increase rapidly. At the same time the movement of events set in which led eventually to their acquiring control of most of the important castles. The members of the Orders were divided into four categories; the Knights, men eligible by birth to bear arms, and having a right to three chargers; the Chaplains; the Serjeants, originally esquires to the knights and having a right to two chargers; and, finally, the Brothers who were of simple birth. The Knights of each Order elected their own Grand Master, who was responsible directly to the Pope. The Military Orders were permitted to draw the sword only when the standard of the cross was displayed, and they wore the same symbol on their surcoats. Their temper differed from that of the feudal knights. The latter, when established in the Holy Land, came to regard the Latin Kingdom as a colonial venture and were ready enough to arrive at a satisfactory relationship with their Saracen neighbours. The Military Orders, on the contrary, often regarded the Muslims with fanaticism, and sometimes tended to resent a period of peace as a sacrilegious interruption of their duties.* The military knights,

* They prosecuted these with great courage. Of the twenty-two Grand Masters of the Temple, prior to the suppression of the Order in 1312, five died in battle, five died of wounds received in battle, and one starved to death in a Saracen prison.

wrote Saint Bernard, 'never dress gaily and wash but seldom. Shaggy by reason of their uncombed hair, they are begrimed with dust, and swarthy from the weight of their armour and the heat of the sun. They do their utmost to possess strong and swift horses, but their mounts are not garnished with ornaments nor decked with trappings, for they think of battle and victory, not of pomp and show. Such hath God chosen for his own, who vigorously and faithfully guard the Holy Sepulchre, all armed with the sword, and most learned in the art of war.'

The Military Orders were nearly matched in importance by the corporations of Italian merchants in the sea-ports. Lodged against a hostile hinterland, both the Armenian and the Latin kingdoms were greatly dependent upon sea power. But neither possessed a navy of its own. For the conveyance of recruits and pilgrims from the West, for the carrying of the trade which provided their main cash revenue, and for protection against the Egyptian fleet, the Christians in the Levant depended upon the galleys of the Italian city states. The latter exacted a heavy payment. In return for their assistance in capturing Tyre, the Venetians received a third of the city and a third of the neighbouring country. At Ayas in Cilicia it was the Genoese, with their special interest in the Mongol trade, who obtained the chief concessions. Up and down the coast the Italian cities extended their privileges and their property, their exemptions from taxes and local laws. Though their policy was solely directed towards acquiring wealth, the Venetians and the Genoese quarrelled as bitterly and nearly as disastrously as the Hospitallers and Templars. Like the Military Orders these corporations of Italian merchants became all but autonomous.

The Italian communities regarded war against the infidel with horror, unless it promised fresh concessions and wider trade. During the two hundred years' occupation of the Holy Land, there were long periods of peace, and others when hostilities were extremely desultory. To speak only of mines and scaling ladders,

14   KRAK OF THE KNIGHTS: One of the vast undercrofts. Similar chambers exist at Margat, Camardesium, and els-
where. See p. 95.

to envisage the castles with portcullis down and ramparts manned, is to create a distorted picture. The inland castles were defensive bastions, but they were also, year in and year out, peacefully busy as centres of feudal administration, the focal points of a number of quiet rural communities. Their Latin rulers on the whole developed—they had to do so—satisfactory relations with the surrounding countrysides, and with the populations (Maronites, Orthodox Muslims, Shi'ites, Druses) upon their territories. Even the Military Orders were not engaged in constant warfare.

The grim and splendid armour of Crusader fortification thus protected a living organism. The life of the castle, in spite of its intense specialization and high degree of discipline, had its religious, social and aesthetic aspects. The masons who built the sheer walls could also produce, where it was needed, decorative carving of the first quality. The castle chapels are tribute to their pacific skill. Windows and portals that might, as at Margat, have come from thirteenth-century France offer a pointed contrast to the austerity of tower, rampart and mountain landscape. The major castles had also their Great Chambers, hung with standards, trophies and tapestries, and sometimes, as at Krak, incorporating fine carving. Fresco and panelling, of which traces remained until recently at Margat, were also used, and Eastern decorative influence had by the thirteenth century become widespread. Wilbrand of Oldenburg describes with delight a chamber, clearly of Arabo-Byzantine inspiration, in the castle at Beirut. 'The floor paved with mosaic', he wrote, 'represents water ruffled by a light breeze, and as one walks one is surprised that one's footsteps leave no trace on the sand that is represented below. The walls of the room are covered with strips of marble which form a panelling of great beauty. The vaulted roof is painted to look like the sky. . . . In the middle of the room is a fountain of marbles in various colours and wonderfully polished. A dragon in the fountain appears to devour a number of animals, represented in mosaic,

5 KRAK OF THE KNIGHTS: The loggia outside the banqueting hall. See Fig. VII, p. 85.

and a limpid and gushing jet of water, with the air that wafts through the open windows, lends the room a delicious freshness.' In such castle chambers the knights grew to appreciate the wailing Arab music—whence the Arabic *al'ud* passed, as lute, into English—and drank the local Syrian wines, such as that vintaged by the Hospitallers at Nephin. These wines, as an Acre inventory of 1266 indicates, were served in goblets of silver and silver-gilt, enamelled and encrusted with precious stones.*

If the atmosphere that prevailed in the Latin castles is to be fully appreciated, it must be realized that a process of assimilation set in from the moment the Franks arrived in the East. They were a small minority, and they were exposed to the persuasions both of climate and landscape, and of alien thought and custom. As early as 1124, King Baldwin II's chaplain wrote: 'We who were Occidentals have now been made Orientals. He who was a Roman or a Frank is now a Galilean. . . . We have already forgotten the places of our birth.' This change was deplored by many, for with assimilation went intermarriage and a dilution of the Frankish blood, of which there was in any case little enough. The offspring of the mixed marriages of the Holy Land, the *Pullani* as they were called, were often unreliable, and the ultimate fall of the Kingdom has been associated, perhaps to an unnecessary extent, with the ever-increasing role which the mixed strain came to play.

There was, however, no combating the various and pervading influences of the East, and the pace of assimilation was often quickened by a deliberate policy of orientalism adopted in high quarters for immediate political ends. Costume was influenced almost from the first. The King of Jerusalem sat cross-legged to receive audience, dressed in a gold-embroidered burnous, and Tancred of Antioch assumed a turban, though for the sake of

* Five years before the fall of Acre at a royal fête that lasted two weeks, the knights and their ladies assumed the characters of the heroes of the Round Table, and outside the city walls, Lancelot, Tristan and Palamede, jousted in the lists.

appearances he pinned the Cross upon it. We hear of the Latins walking in long silk vestments with wide sleeves, trimmed with gold and studded with pearls, and wearing the *kefieh*, or Arab head-dress (from which the West perhaps derived the heraldic mantle). The court, with the introduction of eunuchs, and the approach of suppliants on bended knee, acquired the pomp of the East. Feudal lords kept Arab men-of-letters and Arab doctors— often Lebanese Christians—attached to their castles, while the bourgeoisie began to veil their wives, visit dancing girls, grow beards in the Muslim fashion, and employ paid wailers at their funerals. A knowledge of Arabic became widespread. The Lord of Toron, for instance, acted as interpreter between Richard Cœur de Lion and the Sultan Malek Al-Adel in 1192, and his contemporary, Reynaud de Sagette, was even something of an Arabic scholar.

There were other directions in which of set, and well-set, purpose, everything possible was done to bridge the gap between the Franks and their subjects, and to conciliate local feeling. In the courts, Muslims were permitted to take the oath on the Koran, and in the *Cours de la fonde* which tried commercial and civil suits it was the rule that, in a jury of six, four should be natives. Further, in cases between parties of different race or religion, the only testimony acceptable was that of a witness of the same race or religion as the accused. Thus a Frank hoping to obtain a favourable judgement against a Syrian would have to bring forward Syrian witnesses. It is significant that the Saracen Lord of Shaizar, on the Orontes, could bring a suit against a Frankish noble, and win it. The citizens of the Italian maritime states established in the ports on the coast were quick to grasp that friendly relations with the local communities and with the Saracen merchants of the interior would pay them well. They did everything possible to make the trade and traders of Islam at home in the Latin Kingdom. The Venetians struck coins—*Byzantini Saracenati*—having an

Arabic inscription, a Koranic text, and a date calculated from the Hegira. At Acre, where the accounts of the Customs House were kept in Arabic, and the customs officers spoke the language, a Muslim writer testified that there was no overcharge on merchandise, that the examination of baggage was conducted in a quiet and courteous manner, and that Muslim merchants coming from across the border enjoyed every liberty.

Feudal justice and commercial expediency gained their reward. The caravan traffic, passing along the routes the castles guarded, took a new lease of life; Tyre experienced a prosperity it had hardly known since Phoenician days, and Acre became one of the great ports of the Mediterranean. Ibn Gubayr, a twelfth-century traveller, bears witness, all the more convincing in view of his anti-Christian sentiments, to the general efficiency and prosperity of the Latin Kingdom in the years before the disaster at Hattin. 'We passed', he says, when speaking of his travels in Palestine, 'through a series of villages and cultivated lands all inhabited by the Muslims, who live in great well-being under the Franks. Allah preserve us from such a temptation!' The Franks allow them to keep half of the harvest and limit themselves to the imposition of a poll-tax of 1 dinar and 5 kirats.* Apart from this they only levy a small tax on timber. The Muslims are proprietors of their own houses and run them as they wish. Similar conditions apply along the littoral and in all the districts, towns and villages, inhabited by the Muslims. The majority of them cannot resist the temptation of comparing their lot with that of their brothers in regions under Muslim rule—a lot which is the reverse of agreeable or prosperous. One of the chief tragedies of the Muslims is that they have to complain of the injustices of their own rulers, whereas they cannot but praise the behaviour of the Franks, their natural enemies. May Allah soon put an end to this state of affairs!'

* Considerably less than a like tax imposed on Christians in Muslim territory.

On the frontier, the existence of common boundaries, and the growth of mutual interests, led to contact and co-operation between Saracen and Crusader garrisons. Such contact and co-operation were stimulated on both sides by prolonged captivities, often under fairly generous and agreeable conditions, while awaiting ransom. Raymond III of Tripoli, after eight years with Saladin, developed so cordial a feeling towards his captor that in 1186 he took his part in a quarrel with the King of Jerusalem. The hunting field provided another useful bond. Not only did Latins and Saracens grant each other reciprocal hunting rights, but they frequently organized joint hunting parties. It was presumably on such expeditions that the Franks learnt to use the cheetah, as the Arabs had long done, for the pursuit of gazelle. The memoirs of Usamah Ibn-Munqidh, the Lord of Shaizar, to whom reference has already been made, a poet, warrior and huntsman, give a pleasant picture of the amicable relationships which sometimes prevailed on the frontier. It was to Usamah's uncle that Tancred of Antioch sent a knight with the following letter of recommendation: 'This is a revered knight of the Franks who has completed his pilgrimage and is now on his way back to his country. He has asked me to introduce him to you so that he may see your cavaliers. Accordingly I have sent him to you. Treat him well.'

The castles must often have witnessed such visits and courtesies, which possibly induced a spirit of moderation in subsequent hostilities. They no doubt played their part in those chivalrous episodes which the chroniclers report, as when King Baldwin I, having captured the wife of a great sheikh and learnt she was pregnant, immediately sent her back to her husband with every mark of respect. At one of the sieges of Kerak of Moab, both sides showed to advantage in such an episode. On the marriage of the heir to the fief, meat and wine were sent out to the besieging commander, Saladin, who thereupon tactfully inquired in which tower the bridal pair were lodged, so that he might avoid bombarding it. To pretend that war in the Holy Land was less inhuman than elsewhere would, however, be sentimental. Castellans who, with their garrisons, were in periodic contact across the frontier might develop a mutual respect and understanding, but, as soon as larger stakes and forces were involved, treachery, massacre and the familiar phenomena of war resumed their sway. The ironic and brutal sack of Jerusalem in 1099, and the later massacre of a tenacious Muslim garrison at Tripoli, are to be set to the account of Christian chivalry; while the Sultan Beibars, in spite of his oath, murdered nearly a thousand prisoners after the fall of Saphet in 1266. A comparable massacre of Christians had occurred earlier at Edessa (1144) and the theme was to be repeated at the final fall of Beirut and Acre. Even Saladin's humane and politic clemency, which created something of a legend in Christendom (and was by the Franks naïvely attributed to the existence of a putative Christian mother), had strict limits. After Hattin, he served his thirsty and exhausted prisoners with rose sherbet, but (not without provocation) cut down Reynald de Chatillon with his own sword, and of the Knights of the Orders spared only, and this at the King's express request, the Grand Master of the Temple.

EIGHT

Castles of the Latin Kingdom

Having accounted for the multiplicity and disposition of the Crusader castles, and having outlined their general architectural development, the contacts which they established with the surrounding communities, and the general role they played, it remains to consider in greater detail three of the major castles of the Latin Kingdom. The features and history of these castles—Saone, Krak of the Knights and Chastel Pèlerin—will illustrate both the changes that occurred in military architecture in the East during the twelfth and thirteenth centuries, and the character of the great defensive works built by the Franks. In Chapter Nine some of the major Cilician castles are examined in similar detail.

SAONE

Saone stands in a tangle of wild boulder-strewn hills. The vegetation is scrub and dwarf oak. The approach is by a precipitous track. Only goatherds live in the surrounding country, and the castle that housed Byzantine, Latin and Muslim garrisons, and later a whole town, the capital of an administrative district, is empty. You meet it suddenly, its half-mile of triangular fortification clamped upon a mountain spur. On two sides the ground falls away abruptly into deep ravines. On the third side a vast rock-hewn channel, like a deep wound, isolates the castle from the body of the mountain ridge. This immense channel, nearly 450 feet long and over 60 feet wide, is one of the most impressive memorials that the Latins left in the Holy Land. Its walls, the haunt of the black and scarlet rock-creeper, rise sheer for 90 feet, and the battlements tower above. No drawbridge could span such a channel in a single sweep, and the Crusaders therefore left a needle of solid stone to carry their bridge across. It stands like an obelisk, and recalls those works of the Nile with which this labour of carving some hundred and seventy thousand tons of solid rock alone seems comparable.

Immediately above the rock-channel stands the keep. From its summit the disposition of the castle, shaped like a long isosceles triangle, is best grasped. At the base of the triangle lies the rock-channel, a pool of shadow at all hours except noon. Above it rises the curtain wall, defended by the keep, by three small round towers, and by the round-towered postern whence a bridge, balanced on its needle of rock, spanned the chasm. On the north side of the castle the precipitous ravine must have seemed in itself sufficient defence and the fortifications are negligible. On the south side of the castle are three massive rectangular towers, covering a vulnerable stretch of wall adjoining the rock-channel. Through the last of these towers was contrived the main entrance to the castle. Farther to the west, a second rock-hewn channel, less considerable than the first, divides the body of the castle into two parts. The fortifications beyond it are not imposing and served only to defend an outer bailey, situated at the extremity of the mountain spur. Within the precincts of the eastern and main portion of the castle is to be distinguished the detritus of centuries. The highest ground is covered by the ruins of a Byzantine fortification, the earliest work at Saone, and undoubtedly the whole disposition of the Crusader castle was influenced by earlier Byzantine defences. Post-Crusader history has left a minaret, a bath and the crumbling masonry of an Arab town. Mountain vegetation, laying patient siege, has long since breached the walls and clambers among the wreckage.

The Franks must have taken possession of the Byzantine castle,

16   SAONE: The rock-cut channel and the needle which carried the postern bridge. See above.

raised by the Emperor John Tzimisces late in the tenth century, soon after their arrival in the Holy Land. As a Latin fief, Saone depended on the princedom of Antioch, and its first two feudal lords, father and son, were remarkable. Robert, the father, was Tancred of Antioch's right-hand man, and a redoubtable soldier. He was taken prisoner in 1119 when on an expedition with King Baldwin II against the Atabeg of Damascus. Led before his captor and called upon to accept Islam, he refused. The Atabeg, tucking his robe into his belt, as the chronicler graphically states, drew a sword and cut off the Lord of Saone's head. His body was thrown to the dogs, and his skull, set with jewels, became the Atabeg's drinking cup. William, his son, was in some degree revenged when, with only forty knights, he utterly routed the Emir Dulab and a thousand Seljuk horsemen near Aleppo. William of Saone was a man of wealth and power. He, alone of the ordinary feudal lords, is mentioned with the semi-sovereign princes who later entered into alliance against King Fulk of Jerusalem, and his widow ultimately married the Count of Edessa. It was almost certainly during this William's tenure of the fief of Saone, and probably about 1120, that the important Crusader work was undertaken and that the castle assumed its present shape. Like so many other castles it fell to Saladin after the battle of Hattin. He invested it on June 26, 1188, and brought up a battery of six mangons against the walls. The breaches which these engines effected can be distinguished today, and vast stone balls weighing up to 600 pounds lie within the castle. It appears from the Muslim chroniclers that the Latins fought with great bravery and made at least one sortie. It was probably while this sortie was in progress that the Saracens, scaling the precipitous north-east corner of the walls, found an undefended sector, and broke into the castle. After a bitter struggle, a surviving remnant of the garrison capitulated in the keep and were held to ransom at ten pieces of gold per man. The fortifications were still of considerable strength in the

SAONE: Fortification above the rock-cut channel, showing the early round towers and the bossed masonry. See p. 83.

nineteenth century when they were bombarded by the Egyptian
forces under Ibrahim Pasha.

The fact that this key-castle, never recaptured after 1188,
remained for less than a century in Crusader hands, was a
grave matter for the Latins. It has proved providential to the
student of Crusader building, as Saone is consequently the

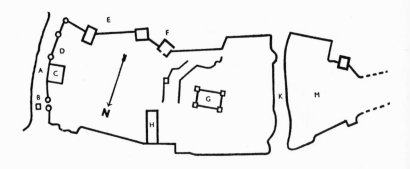

VI · SAONE

A: Rock-cut channel. B: Bridge needle. C: Keep. D: Small
round towers. E: Rectangular towers on vulnerable southern
face. F: Gate Tower. G: Byzantine fortress. H: Cistern. K:
Rock divide. M: Lower Ward of elongated shape (stretching a
quarter-mile farther west than shown on plan).

finest and best-preserved example of the early castles of the Latin
Kingdom. The masonry at Saone is massive and, as so often in
early Crusader work, is heavily and roughly bossed. It presents
after eight hundred years a striking contrast to the decayed walls of
the tenth-century castle of the Byzantines. Other features indica-
tive of an early date, apart from the general design of the castle,
are the shape and small salient of the three large rectangular
towers on the south wall; the fact that two of these towers and
the keep have no direct communication with the curtain; and,
finally, the general absence of loopholes in the body of walls and

towers, so that effective defence is for the most part confined to the wall tops, while even there the merlons are not pierced for fire. Two at least of these features seem to indicate Byzantine influence, an influence also visible in the fact that part of the wall-walk is carried on corbelling. The arrangement by which the main gate is placed in a re-entrant angle in one of the large rect-angular towers is one of the earliest examples of a bent entrance extant in the Levant. As for the great rock-channel, it is a triumph-antly ambitious development of the ditch which the Byzantines habitually set to protect the approaches to their castles.

Since dating from the first half of the twelfth century, the keep is, naturally enough, of the solid square type then going up all over Europe. It measures externally 80 feet square, and the outer wall, facing the rock-channel, is over 16 feet thick. The stairs are placed in the depth of an interior wall, and it has a single narrow door—it was defended by a portcullis—giving on the courtyard of the castle. Where it differs from the large European keeps of the period is in its relatively lower height. That it has only two storeys like the Crusader keeps at Subeibe, Gibelet and elsewhere, is probably due to the prevailing timber shortage which meant that vaulting was necessary throughout. In both chambers at Saone the vaulting is carried on a huge central pier, analogous to piers used for the same purpose at Krak and Subeibe.

In the curtain over the rock-channel are three small round towers. These are possibly the earliest round towers built by the Latins in the Holy Land. If two of them were not clearly con-temporary with the main Crusader work, it might be reasonable to assign them to a later date than *c*. 1120. One of the towers is solid masonry in its lower portion, a type of construction found in early medieval fortification, and another is provided with only two loopholes. The third, which was probably damaged, and was rebuilt at a later date, is equipped with seven loopholes, and well illustrates the change of attitude which led to the provision of loopholes throughout the full height of a wall or tower, making active defence possible on every level.

KRAK OF THE KNIGHTS

Between the southernmost slopes of Gebel Alawi and the first steep ramparts of the Lebanon, the Nahr el-Kebir, the Eleutherus of antiquity, waters a fertile plain.* Known to the Crusaders as 'la Bocquée', this plain offers the sole practicable channel of communication between the Tripoli coast on the west, and, to the east, the valley of the Orontes, Homs, Hama and the inland deserts. To guard this dangerous gap in the natural defences of the coastal belt, the Crusaders built no less than five castles: Krak, Akkar, and nearer to the sea, Arima, Chastel Rouge and Safita. Incomparably the strongest of these castles was Krak of the Knights, the most remarkable example of the military architecture of the twelfth and thirteenth centuries, and, in the opinion of Lawrence, 'perhaps the best preserved and most wholly admirable castle in the world'.

With strong natural defences on three sides, the great pile stands on a spur of the Gebel Alawi, dominating the plain below. The surrounding hills are wild and have something of moorland character. The views are immense. Here was situated before the Crusades the small 'Castle of the Kurds', which the Latins occupied definitively in 1110. They began soon after to replace it by the vast castle which for over a century and a half, in the phrase of a Muslim writer, stuck like a bone in the very throat of the Saracens. The latter on at least twelve occasions in vain beleaguered it. In 1142 the Count of Tripoli, doubtless finding the

---

* Parts of the Gebel Alawi were for much of the Crusading period in the hands of the Ismailis (the 'Assassins' of the Crusading chronicles). They were usually in alliance with the Franks, and their chief strongholds were the castles of Kadmus and Masiaf.

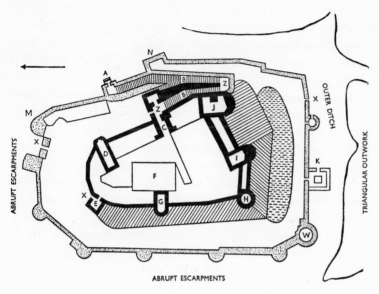

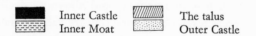

VII · KRAK OF THE KNIGHTS

Plan showing the relationship of the Inner and Outer Wards.

■ Inner Castle	▨	The talus
▤ Inner Moat	▢	Outer Castle

X: Postern. A: Main Gate. B: Passage leading up covered ramp past exposed elbows at Z. C: Main Gate to Inner Ward. D: Chapel. F: Loggia and Refectory. H: Warden's Tower, constituting with linked towers at I and J the south strongwork. K: Arab work of post-Crusader period. The towers at W, M and N were also rebuilt by the Arabs. The rectangular fortification incorporated at D, E and G dates from the earlier twelfth century castle. On the south the talus was known as 'the Mountain'.

charge of so important a castle more than he could support, gave it into the keeping of the Hospitallers. It was during their tenure that Krak of the Knights became the foremost bastion of the Holy Land, and a regular point of convergence for expeditions

against the Muslim interior. In 1163 the Emir Nur ed-Din and his
besieging army, surprised during the noon siesta, suffered a
grave defeat beneath the walls, and Saladin, a generation later,
having inspected the strength of the defences, withdrew without
attempting a siege.

After the departure of Saint Louis in 1254, the decadence of the
Latin Kingdom set in, and Krak began for the first time to experience serious difficulties. The campaigns of the Sultan Beibars, that
ruthless and efficient general, known to his contemporaries as 'the
Panther', systematically reduced the extent of Crusader territory.
Saphet fell in 1266, Jaffa and Antioch in 1268. Only parts of the
coastal belt and a few strong points remained. All the hinterland
towards Hama and the Orontes, over which Krak had once
exercised suzerainty, was now hostile territory, and the castle
became a lonely outpost. Yearly the Saracens ventured with
greater impunity beneath the walls, and communications grew
more hazardous. In 1268 Hughes Revel, the Grand Master of the
Hospitallers, wrote an eloquent and pathetic letter revealing the
plight of the castle. He speaks of inadequate resources, revenues
shrunken with loss of territory, and above all decline in manpower. Whereas Krak early in the century had maintained a garrison of 2,000, in 1268 Krak and Margat together, the sole fortresses
of importance that survived inland, could muster only some 300
knights.

Three years after the dispatch of this letter, on March 3, 1271,
the Sultan Beibars with an Egyptian army, and the contingents of
the Grand Master of the Assassins, and of the Emirs of Homs and
Saone, invested the castle. It was to prove the last and fatal siege.
The fighting monks who constituted the strength of the garrison
were seasoned warriors, and, as the Muslim chroniclers testify,
fought with tenacity; but they were no more than a handful. On
March 5 they withdrew from the *burgus*, or walled suburb, of
which no trace remains. The triangular outwork to the south of the

castle was next invested. It was a fortification of little strength, but incessant rain delayed operations and the Crusaders were not evicted until March 21. The serious siege of the castle then began with an attack on the outer curtain. The south-west tower (marked W in Fig. vii) was successfully mined and collapsed on the 29th of March. The Muslims storming into the outer ward surprised and killed a number of the garrison who had no time to withdraw, though the peasantry, sheltering in the ward, were spared. The besiegers now found themselves facing the formidable inner defences at their most imposing point. They may well have been dismayed. Having forced three outer lines of defence, they were confronted with a fourth which seemed impregnable. The chroniclers make no mention of active siege in the following days, and it seems that Beibars, despairing of force, had recourse to trickery. A forged letter was conveyed into the castle, purporting to come from the Grand Commander at Tripoli. It instructed the knights to surrender. They did so, and the castle that had held for 161 years fell on the 8th of April, the knights leaving under safe-conduct for the coast.

If Beibars were to return he would find Krak almost as formid-able as it was 700 years ago. Chance, the solidity of the Crusader building,* and the meticulously faithful restorations recently undertaken by the French, have preserved it almost intact. The castle, built on a strictly concentric plan, has two lines of defence, the second or inner ward, on higher ground, at every point dominating the outer. The walls of the outer ward are particularly impressive on the west and north, where the curtain is furnished with box-machicoulis (in small part of Latin construction) and a series of powerful round towers calculated to give fully effective

---

* The masonry is massive throughout and usually of the finest quality. The stone courses of the inner ward average 1¾ feet in height, and the blocks are often as much as a yard long. The core of the walls, following the usual medieval practice, is of rubble and mortar.

flanking fire. These towers are pierced with loopholes, having stirrup-shaped bases, and so set that no two loopholes are directly one above the other. The merlons on the wall-walk are also furnished with loopholes. The castle is liberally supplied with entrances and posterns (two of the latter being set in the re-entrant angle of a tower), thus enabling the garrison to make sorties or receive messages with comparative ease. The main entrance on the east front is highly impressive: the wide ramped and vaulted passage, that leads into the heart of the castle, contains three elbows, and was defended by a drawbridge and external moat, by machicoulis, by four gates, and by at least one portcullis. The outer girdle of walls, and the ramped entrance, are for the most part Hospitaller work dating from the late twelfth century, and they show clearly enough the change, and advance, in the science of fortification that took place after about 1170.

The inner or second series of fortifications assumed their present shape a little later, but they incorporated an earlier Crusader castle, probably contemporary with Saone. Most of the rectangular towers of this first castle were rebuilt by the Hospitallers as round towers, but some of the earliest construction stands (e.g. the rectangular work at C, D, E and G, in the plan on p. 85), and there remains rough bossage characteristic of early work. The most striking features of the inner fortifications, as reshaped in the late twelfth century, are the gigantic taluses on the south and west, and the splendid redoubt on the south, a formidable mass of masonry composed of three huge linked towers.

From the summit of the redoubt the size and cunning of Krak can be fully appreciated. The sensation, as the wind whistles over the battlements, is not unlike that of being on the bridge of a ship, and the fortress seems to ride above the extended landscape with a ship's poise and mastery. There is the same strength, together with the same precision of design that, transcending the utilitarian, creates a work of art. The plan of the concentric walls, the

18 KRAK OF THE KNIGHTS: Aerial view from the north-west. See p. 84.

skilful disposition of the flanking towers, the calculated relationship of each part of the whole, are infinitely pleasing, and are contrived with the exactitude and economy of a naval architect's blue-
print. The sense of unity, of a directing intelligence, is one which
a ship and a well-conceived building both pre-eminently convey.

On its south side, where natural defences are lacking, the
redoubt slopes away into a monstrous talus, 80 feet thick, and
known to the besieging Muslims as 'the Mountain'. This talus
plunges into a moat so considerable as to be almost a small lake.
Beyond rises the south wall of the outer curtain, defended by a
substantial square tower (the latter built by the Arabs after 1271).
Beyond the outer curtain lies a dry moat and a triangular outwork
whose defences have disappeared. In the south-west tower of the
redoubt, from whose summit the standard of the Hospital was
displayed, is situated the airy chamber of the Grand Master of the
Order, whose delicate pilasters, Gothic vaulting, and decorative
frieze, date from 1230–40. Here the wardens of the castle, whose
names—Pierre de Mirmande, Armand de Montbrun, Hughes
Revel, Nicolas Lorgne—speak of France, elaborated policy,
directed administration, and looked down on the living body of
the castle. Below, in the Romanesque chapel, moving in its
monastic simplicity, Geoffrey de Joinville, the uncle of the
chronicler, was buried. He seemed to his brother knights the true
pattern of medieval chivalry, and Richard Cœur de Lion, in token
of his respect, granted him the arms of England to quarter with
his own. In the great Chamber, with its adjacent loggia (reminiscent, in its stone tracery, of some work at Rheims), banquets were
held and counsel was taken. In the courtyard came and went the
challenging figures, the Raymonds, the Tancreds, the Bohemunds,
that loom more than life-size in the annals of Crusading history,
and one day the King of Hungary arrived, bringing with him as a
gift in perpetuity the rents of large Hungarian estates.

Today, Krak of the Knights, so perfectly preserved, seems

KRAK OF THE KNIGHTS: from the south-west. See above.
KRAK OF THE KNIGHTS: The lower courtyard.

incongruously empty, its silence hardly natural. The windmill that stood upon the north wall should be grinding corn; in the huge vaulted chamber (130 yards long), that must once have housed the men-at-arms, troops should be quartered; the cry of the watch should echo along the battlements, and in the halls and passages the clank of mailed knights; the guardroom should be noisy with medieval French, and from the chapel should come the chant of the Latin mass. Instead there are only the shadows of the kestrels cruising above, and the sun-scorched stones.

CHASTEL PÈLERIN

Near the modern town of Haifa, Carmel's rocky spine brings the mountain system of inland Palestine to within a stone's throw of the Mediterranean. No comparable coastal pass intervenes between Acre and the deserts of Egypt. Some miles south of this pass, a conveniently isolated promontory, about 270 yards long and a 160 yards wide, juts into the sea. Here in 1218, with the help of the Teutonic Knights, and of energetic pilgrims (whose labours the name of the castle commemorates), the Templars built *Castrum Peregrinorum*.

Chastel Pèlerin, as the Franks called it, has been badly damaged. In the nineteenth century, Ibrahim Pasha took away ship-loads of masonry to rebuild Acre, and the site continued for decades afterwards to be little more than a builder's quarry. None the less the fragmented castle is imposing in its ruin. Upon the masonry, gulls, indifferent to the aura of history, stand sentinel on webbed feet. The waves splash the lapsing walls; sand drifts into the vaulted chambers and has filled the moat. Stilts and dunlins in compact flocks scud over a strip of marshy ground inland, beyond shimmer grey olive trees, and in the background rise the rocky slopes of Mount Carmel. Two sandy and steeply-shelving bays flank the

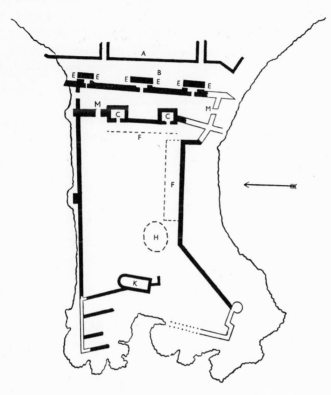

VIII · CHASTEL PÈLERIN

A: Counterscarp. B: Ditch. C: Great Towers. E: Posterns.
F: Vaults. H: Templar Church. K: Vaulted Hall. M: Gates.

promontory and ruins. They once offered good anchorage to Genoese and Venetian vessels.

Like Tortosa, and like no other of the great castles, Chastel Pèlerin was never taken by siege. Two years after it was completed the Sultan Malek el Moaddhem attacked it with a large force, and brought up a trebuchet, three petraries, and four mangons, to bombard the walls. He was unable, however, to pierce the main defences. The Templars had formidable artillery of their own, under the direction of a special corps of 300 men, and they rapidly put out of action the trebuchet and a petrary. The castle, moreover, as rarely happened during the Crusades, was heavily garrisoned. The Grand Master of the Temple arrived to superintend the defence, and contingents sailed in from Acre and Cyprus in response to the papal legate's appeal for reinforcements. After a month's fruitless and costly endeavour, the Sultan abandoned the siege. His casualties included three emirs and 200 mameluks.

The Emperor Frederick II, when in Palestine, approved the strength of Chastel Pèlerin, coveted the place, and tried in 1229, by a sudden manœuvre, to wrest it from the Templars. The monks, no doubt aware of the Emperor's reputation, were perhaps forewarned. At all events, when Frederick entered the castle, they immediately closed the gates behind him. He was held a virtual prisoner until he renounced all pretensions to the stronghold. A generation later (1250–51), Saint Louis when at Acre installed his Queen, Margaret of Provence, in the safety of the castle. It was there that she gave birth to the Comte d'Alençon, among whose godfathers was the warden of the castle. During the subsequent decline of Frankish power, the Saracens razed the considerable town—it had its bourgeois court of justice—that had grown up outside the castle walls, and cut the standing timber (1265), but the castle itself was impervious to attack. There came at last the fatal spring and summer of 1291. Tyre fell on May 19, and Acre on May 23. Beirut and the *Château de Mer* at Sidon, capitulated in July. Eventually Chastel Pèlerin remained the sole Christian territory in the Holy Land. With the loss of the Kingdom, however, the reason for such a bastion was gone. On August 14 the Templars evacuated the castle and embarked for Cyprus.*

---

* The Muslims did not occupy the castle until some two or three months later. The fortified island of Ruad, off Tortosa, held out until 1303.

The fortifications at Chastel Pèlerin offer in almost every respect a striking contrast to those at Krak of the Knights. There are, with two inconsiderable exceptions, no round towers of Crusader date,* while the position of the castle adequately accounts for the fact that there is no attempt at concentric fortification, and that nowhere, except on the east or landward side, is there careful provision for lines of fire. On three sides the rocky promontory, wading deep into the waves, offered in itself a strong protection to a garrison who were also masters of the sea. On three sides therefore the Templars confined themselves to building a single massive wall rising almost from the water's edge, with one or two rectangular towers. Little of this work remains, except on the north where a stretch of wall and part of two towers are standing. Wisely the main defences were piled up on the landward side of the promontory. They are still impressive, and this largely by reason of the cyclopean stones of which they were built. Chastel Pèlerin was a Phoenician site and the Crusaders utilized the ancient masonry that they found on the spot, masonry that dwarfs even the stonework at Krak. Many of the blocks are 4 feet long by 2 feet high, and the chroniclers record that a single yoke of oxen could hardly transport them. These gigantic stones are carefully drafted and bossed, and bedded in a very thin cement, compounded in part of powdered sea-shells. The core of the walls is an exceptionally hard rubble.

The series of defences that protect the landward face of Chastel Pèlerin are complex, and represent perhaps the fullest Crusader development of a conception of fortification associated with the Byzantine cities. An attacking force would encounter, first, a solid masonry glacis, and a ditch or moat (80 feet wide and 20 feet deep), which could be flooded from the sea at either end, and which

---

* The Templars showed a preference for rectangular fortification, but the use of ready-dressed Phoenician masonry at Chastel Pèlerin (see plate 28) would go a long way to account for the avoidance of circular towers.

apparently also contained fresh-water springs. Beyond lay the first curtain, 50 feet high and 20 feet thick, stretching the whole width of the promontory. It was provided with a vaulted *chemin de ronde* and strengthened by three rectangular towers. From the former opened at regular intervals casemates in the thickness of the wall, roomy enough to hold at least four men—two working the loophole, and two acting as relief.* There was apparently no machicolation. The three towers, which were 90 feet broad and had a 30-foot salient, appear to have contained posterns, some of which were furnished with portcullises. Behind this first curtain lay a second whose main features were two enormous rectangular towers, linked with a covered corridor inside the curtain. One of these, which still stands to a height of 110 feet and dominates the ruins, had three floors, the two lower with barrel vaults, and the loftier top storey with fine rib vaults. It is worth noting that the exposed face of this tower is a good deal thinner than parts of the curtain wall. This is a weakness not uncommon in Byzantine fortification, and one which the builders of Krak would certainly have avoided at so vital a point.

The frontal fire from this twin line of defences was nicely calculated, and must, with walls and towers fully manned, have been exceptionally powerful. The large towers of the inner curtain alternate with those of the outer curtain, so that the volume of fire from the towers would be evenly distributed. The outer curtain, covering the ditch, the counterscarp, and the ground beyond, has the maximum elevation possible without interfering with the fire from the inner curtain and the great towers. A besieging force was thus subjected to a double line of fire, from five towers and two curtains. The great towers not only dominate the forward curtain but command an easy view of the plain beyond

* Such casemates reduced the strength of the wall. In the outer ward of Krak they were only inserted in the west wall, where, owing to the lie of the land, heavy siege engines could not be used.

and the coast running up to the foot of Mount Carmel. In the dry climate of the Levant, a cloud of dust would have betrayed to the watch the approach of an army while still many miles distant.

The buildings in the interior of the castle, where the Queen of France lodged, supposedly in proper state and comfort, have nearly all disappeared. There are a number of large vaulted chambers, presumably used for storage purposes, running nearly the whole length of the inner curtain, and others on the south side of the castle. Bishop Pococke, the English eighteenth-century traveller, saw, though already ruined, 'a fine lofty church of ten sides, built in a light Gothic taste', having three apsidal chapels of hexagonal shape. Little now remains beyond part of an apsidal chapel, but the church was clearly, like the Temple church in London, the church in the Templar monastery at Thomar in Portugal, and others, copied after the church in the Temple enclosure at Jerusalem, known as the Dome of the Rock.

The day in 1291 when the last Latin vessel drew anchor at Chastel Pèlerin, sailing for Cyprus, marks the true end of the Crusades. It was an end that had been inevitable since the departure of Saint Louis nearly two generations earlier. From that date the Franks had lost not only the strategic but the moral initiative. In the eleventh century they found an Arab world in decline, and came with much to give; but eventually, and perhaps inevitably, the transplanted civilization of medieval France ran to seed. Crusader architecture, both civil and military, remains however to prove the poise and vigour which this civilization retained for well over a century on foreign soil. The great castles, though merely instruments of war and administration, were in their conception and execution worthy of the genius that presided over the rise of contemporary ecclesiastical building in the West.

Cilician Castles

Two or three generations before the fall of Acre the Armenians understood their impending fate. The rising tide of Muslim advance was beating against their mountain ramparts both in the north and in the south. When Leo II died in 1219 he left a competent army and a number of impressive fortifications which had recently been reconstructed or strengthened. His successor continued his extensive building programme and granted further fiefs to the Hospitallers and the Teutonic Knights. In short, though split by faction as always, the Armenians did all that they could to strengthen their defences. But a serious defeat in the last year of Leo II's reign showed that their unaided resources were not enough and that they must seek help elsewhere.

The Latin states were themselves too hard pressed to be of any assistance. Only in the second half of the fourteenth century when a branch of the Lusignans had acquired the throne of Armenia was a little help forthcoming from Cyprus. The Holy Roman Emperor, whose vassal the King of Armenia was, sent evasive messages but no troops. The Popes were anxious to support the last remaining Christian foothold on the mainland but found little answering enthusiasm amongst the secular rulers of the West. Nor were the people and clergy of the Armenian kingdom ever prepared to honour the promises of a reformation in the calendar their kings made to please Rome. Ultimately the Armenians were driven to pin their hopes on fabulous stories of the Mongol hordes turning Christian. It was not altogether a vain hope. Christian Mongols did indeed for a short space capture most of Syria. The Armenian king is said to have travelled across Asia to

96

21 LAMPRON: The apartments at the end of the inner ward. See p. 38.

the court of the Great Khan and to have been appointed by him as his chief political adviser on western affairs. But it all came to nothing. The Great Khan was preoccupied with difficulties 2,000 miles from Cilicia, and there was no prospect of achieving the Crusade from Europe, which he demanded should act in concert with his own attack on the Saracens.

When the vision of Mongol support faded there was nothing left but once again to strengthen the fortifications. Building went on well into the fourteenth century. The western sea-ports in particular were enlarged or reconstructed, often with help from Cyprus or the Italian cities. Thus the latest of the Cilician castles, such as those at Anamur and Aghliman, have links with Renaissance Italy.

The strategic sites in Cilicia have been valued and used by Arabs, Byzantines, Armenians, Franks and Turks. It is hardly surprising therefore that the Cilician castles exhibit in themselves the development of medieval fortification. We have already seen (p. 46) that Azgit stands for a type of Byzantine fortification common in Cilicia. Later development is typified by two Armenian and two Frankish castles.

SIS

Like the back of a sea monster, a long sharp ridge protrudes from the mass of the Taurus mountains into the Cilician plain. Standing at the southern end of one of the main routes into the Taurus, it was a good site for the capital of Cilicia. Leo II chose it as such and crowned the entire summit of the ridge with fortifications. As with most twelfth-century Armenian work the site largely determines the shape and character of the castle. The architect's object was to co-operate with nature rather than to impose upon the site a preconceived ideal. The consequence is total asymmetry.

2 SIS: The lower ward. One of the gates is in the shadow of the tower on the right. The curtain wall on the left has two rows of loopholes. See p. 99.

3 ILAN: Gate to the upper ward showing the bent entrance between flanking towers. See pp. 51, 102.

Wherever the cliffs could be scaled or the defence given an opportunity to strike at the besiegers, there are walls and towers, mostly with battlements and loopholes. Elsewhere nature provided the ramparts. The lower part of the walls are usually built against rock. Because of this and the extreme unsuitability of the ground for siege engines, the Armenian walls are a good deal thinner than contemporary Frankish work, and in many places they are little more than breastworks to defend a man standing on the ground within. The towers are accommodated to the shape of the ground, but a rounded type is clearly preferred. Lower wards are added at the base of the main ridge where the slope is easier. The ground is rocky and uneven and it is difficult for a besieger close to the castle to get a clear view of how the defences lie. He is therefore liable to be surprised by sudden sallies through postern gates of which there are a number.

The weak point of Sis is a col which divides the smaller, southern part of the ridge from the much longer and sharper northern portion. But both parts of the ridge have been provided with defences facing each other across the col and each could hold out independently. Behind the defences to the north there is a considerable range of ruined living-quarters and a subterranean vaulted cistern with two aisles. This is supplemented by a number of smaller cisterns. The entrance to the southern part of the ridge has two gates close together, each with a corridor behind it. The purpose of this unique arrangement is not certain. Perhaps one of the gates was originally an entrance to a tower now destroyed, or perhaps it was meant to confuse attackers. Behind the entrance corridors lie the ruins of a building which was both a royal apartment and the strongest point in the castle. The building culminated in a massive round tower occupying the whole width of the ridge and dropping sheer to a rock moat, which divides its base from an outer ward running to the end of the summit ridge.

The approaches to the col itself were skilfully defended. The western side of the ridge being precipitous the only approach is from the east. Here the curtain wall, following the contours of the col, swing inwards towards the centre of the col, forming a cul-de-sac. Within this cul-de-sac there are two gates, one on either hand. An attack on one of the gates would be exposed to fire from three sides and to the risk of a sortie through the other.

IX · SIS

A: Main gate. B: Gate to south-eastern ward. C and D: Gates to inmost ward. E: Royal apartments. F: Rock moat. G: Underground cistern. X: Postern gates. The castle extends a quarter-mile farther to the north than is shown on the plan.

The main entrance, that on the northern side of the cul-de-sac, is protected by box machicolation and gives access to a covered passage closed by a second gate. It is moreover tucked into the side of a tower in such a way that it is almost impossible to use a battering ram against it. The gate on the opposite side of the cul-de-sac is in the lee of a tower. In the adjoining curtain wall commanding the approach to the col excellent provision has been made for archers.

It was on these eastern approaches to the col that fierce fighting occurred during the final siege. Under cover of fire from balistas stationed on the curtain wall the garrison made a sortie against the besieging Mameluk force. The fighting was inconclusive and discontent fanned by the near approach of famine affected the loyalty of the garrison. Traitors who were in communication with the enemy infiltrated into the special guard about the king's person. One night, having determined to seize the king, they gained admittance to the royal apartments. Only the loyalty of a few saved Leo VI. While some of them held the door to his chamber, a Greek warrior in charge of the castle's war engines lowered the king by rope to the rock moat whence he gained the outer ward and was able to organize the recovery of the royal apartments.

The castle held out for some days longer, but at length famine and renewed discontent within the walls forced Leo to capitulate. This was the end of the kingdom of Cilicia. When the news reached Cairo, drums were beaten for three days.

ILAN

The mysterious atmosphere of Ilan, and its evil reputation for snakes and sorcery, no doubt derive from its setting: the landscape is sombre, and the muddy waters of the Ceyhan sweep in a wide loop round the rocky ridge on which the castle stands. Atmosphere here can owe nothing to the past, for Ilan has no history. Even its medieval name has been forgotten, though it seems improbable that so fine a castle can have escaped the attention of the chroniclers. The difficulty is a common one in Cilicia. New names have come into being, and the old names mentioned in the chronicles can often no longer be attached to any definite place.

Evidence suggests that Ilan did not belong to one of the great barons and was therefore probably a royal castle or controlled by one of the Military Orders. Its architecture, like that of Tumlu, a neighbouring castle very similar in style (which also cannot be clearly identified in the Crusading chronicles), marks it as Armenian work. Probably both castles were built by Leo II (1186–1219).

Ilan is indeed an outstanding example of Armenian military architecture, which, though derived from Byzantine work, is

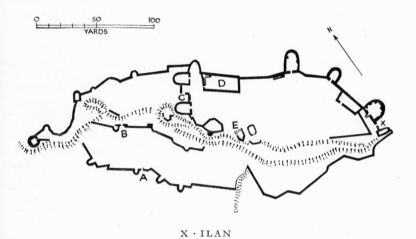

X · ILAN

A: Gate to lower ward. B: Gate to middle ward. C: Gate to upper ward. D: Cistern. E: Chapel. X: Postern gate.

distinctive in itself. The castle is characteristically set upon the summit of a rock ridge. The architect has accommodated his walls to the sinuosities of the ground with masterly effect. The ridge, though steep, is by no means unclimbable but the walls have been sited so as to push an attacker out on to the steepest slopes. This has been done so cleverly that the castle almost defends itself without a garrison, though the twists and turns of the walls do in fact provide the defenders with admirable bastions from which to direct flanking fire against an attacking force.

The core of the castle is an upper ward on the summit of the ridge. Below lie a middle and a lower ward covering the side on which approach is easiest. Thus to gain the core of the castle it is necessary to pass through three gates. The first two have typical Armenian double arches with space between for machicolation and each is placed in the lee of a round tower. A barbican defends the approach to the upper ward. The gate is set deep between horseshoe-shaped towers, and the entrance makes two right-angle turns, the first below machicolation. The upper ward contains a tiny chapel showing the remains of fresco, a subterranean cistern furnished with a flight of steps, and solidly built living-quarters. Concealed between two towers set close together there is a narrow postern.

The seven horseshoe towers of the upper ward are the chief glory of Ilan. Their shape is characteristically Armenian and so is their masonry, well squared and laid in neat courses but with the face left rough or bossed, for the stone is of great hardness. The individual blocks are generally larger than Byzantine work in Cilicia, but smaller than most of the Frankish masonry in Syria. The towers have a notably bold projection which enables them thoroughly to outflank a besieger at the foot of the walls. They are provided with a number of loopholes at different levels with sharply splayed feet to allow an archer to cover the ground near the walls. The two entrance towers are a formidable unit, being linked together by a gallery above the entrance without any communication with the curtain wall on either side. The two towers at the opposite end of the ridge are similarly cut off from communication with the curtain.

In view of these massive defences, admirably calculated to take a heavy toll of any besieging force, it is not surprising that Ilan seems unmarked by siege warfare. Perhaps it finally capitulated through famine or perhaps the prospect of waiting for this inevitable end with no hope of relief caused the garrison to evacuate the castle at the approach of a besieging army.

CAMARDESIUM

The castle of Camardesium above Silifke seems, unlike Ilan, a happy and hopeful place. Below it is the Mediterranean and on the horizon lies Cyprus.

The castle occupies the summit of a hill of even steepness on every side, enough to disconcert but not to deter a determined

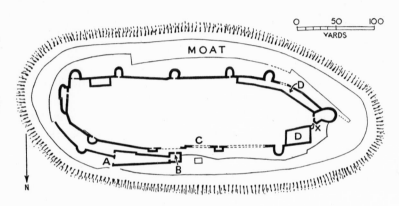

XI · CAMARDESIUM

A: Entrance ramp. B: First gate. C: Probable site of main gate.
D: Undercrofts. X: Postern gate.

attack. The site, of a type rare in the big Crusading castles, called for defences equally strong all round. It is impossible to say what solution the original Byzantine architects proposed, for their work was entirely swept away by the Hospitallers who acquired the town and castle as a gift from Leo II in 1210. The military order probably began to rebuild immediately for an unusual congregation of Hospitaller leaders is known to have been there about this date. The horseshoe shape of most of the towers suggests Armenian or Byzantine inspiration. At any rate it is a characteristic

Cilician shape which is not found frequently in Syria or Palestine. The castle has but a single line of defence. The strength of this is greatly enhanced by a wide and deep moat lined with masonry which surrounds the whole castle. This would have made mining difficult and, although the moat must have been dry, it would be a considerable obstacle to an attack. The entrance to the castle is up a ramp which begins in the moat. An outwork with a round tower is placed so as to take in the rear anyone advancing up this ramp. A square tower with box machicolation over the entrance stands at the head of the ramp. The entrance is bent and issues from the tower directly beneath the main curtain wall. The gate into the castle itself has been destroyed. Traces suggest it was probably a little to the west and that the entrance led through one or more chambers as at Til Hamdoun.

The interior of the castle is now strewn with the ruined masonry of a chapel and a range of living apartments. To judge from the sweep of the remaining vaults they were of a fineness comparable with Krak of the Knights. And as at Krak and Til Hamdoun there remains a spacious undercroft whose utility is obvious in these extremes of climate. There are also a number of cisterns above and below ground. All the buildings within the castle are built of relatively small stones beautifully drafted and squared. But what is most remarkable is the way in which the stones of the towers and the curtain wall taper so that their inner face, embedded in the cement and rubble filling, is less than half the outer face. It is as if the stones were teeth putting down tapering roots into the filling of the walls. This unusual system must have strengthened the cohesion of the wall.

Apart from its size, the most striking things about Camardesium are the horseshoe towers. They have a truly aggressive intention. Each projects far beyond the curtain wall and they outflank any attack which might scale the scarp of the moat. They are set close enough together to give each other valuable support, and

24 CAMARDESIUM: The Hospitaller walls. See abov
25 CAMARDESIUM: Square entrance tower at the head of the ramp. S above.

a number of tall loopholes, with sharply splayed feet, make excellent provision for archers. Apart from one flight of stairs from the courtyard, the wall-walk can only be reached by stairs within the towers, and each tower was provided with an inner gate. Thus, if assailants burst into the castle they might be quite unable to get at the defenders on the wall unless they succeeded in taking a tower. The wall-walk is an excellent broad fighting platform and, on the south side at any rate, both the curtain wall and the towers were provided with continuous machicolation. Most of the fighting was probably done from the wall-walk, for only from there could the bottom of the moat be covered.

In short, Camardesium is an exceptionally powerful castle designed to give the garrison every opportunity of striking back at their besiegers. It is hard therefore to accept at face value the pathetic tale which the chroniclers tell of its voluntary surrender by the Hospitallers. Only a few years after Leo II had given the castle to the Order, his daughter Isabella, who had become queen in his stead, sought refuge with the Hospitallers at Camardesium from the Regent Constantine who was trying to force her to marry his son. Rather than let it be said that they had given up the daughter of their benefactor, the Hospitallers chose to surrender the whole castle. Isabella eventually married Constantine's son and found him better than she had expected.

ANAMUR

As the Cilician castles show, the main line of development in Crusading fortification was towards the multiplication of lines of defence and of devices to surprise the besieger and economize in manpower. All the subtlety of architects and masons was employed in making defence aggressive, a policy clearly shown in those castles which are perhaps the latest Frankish works in the

6 ANAMUR: The castle from the top of the fourteen-sided tower. See p. 106.

7 ANAMUR: The towers of the land ward. See p. 106.

Levant. Set upon the most southerly beach in Turkey, Anamur
was intended to defend a lush plain enclosed upon every side
except the south by a tangle of mountains. A huge fourteen-sided

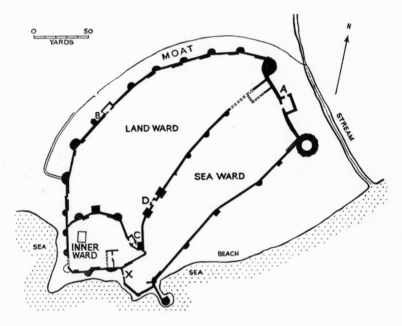

XII · ANAMUR

A : Gate to sea ward. B : Gate to land ward. C : Gate to inner
ward. D : Gate between land and sea wards. X : Postern gate.

tower dominates the beach. Its rows of meurtrieres or loopholes
are menacing, and in the adjoining curtain wall there are galleries
at two levels and a wall-walk, each furnished with loopholes both
to the outside and to the interior of the castle. The curious towers,
resembling Kentish oast-houses, which look across the moat to
the distant mountains are set close together. The whole castle
bristles with towers—there are thirty-six of them—and each is

furnished with splayed loopholes. The wall-walk is also a formidable fighting platform and is a little lower than the towers. The
castle is divided into three wards. The inner one is built on rock
and is considerably higher than either the land or the sea ward.
The latter is the weakest part of the castle. The wall and gate
dividing it from the land ward are fortified wholly against attack
from the sea and could not be defended against an enemy who had
penetrated the land ward. At one end of the sea ward, there is a
postern gate pierced through the rock, giving access to a tiny
cove which is otherwise inaccessible. It was the garrison's private
port. Three of the other gates are each bent entrances set in square
towers. It is interesting that a few of the battlements are of a
distinctive type found nowhere else in Cilicia but common in
Italian castles of the fourteenth and fifteenth centuries.

Going from tower to tower, through the galleries in the curtain
wall, up the stairs of the fourteen-sided tower, one expects the
chink of armour, the sound of voices, but all is silence. It is five
centuries since the last Lusignan knights boarded ship in their
private harbour and left for Cyprus.

TEN

The Withdrawal to Cyprus

In 1291, when the last garrison on the mainland abandoned Chastel Pèlerin and sailed for Cyprus, the island had long been a Frankish kingdom. A century earlier Richard Cœur de Lion had seized it, with little pretext from the Byzantines.* He sold it almost at once to the Templars, and 120 of them, horse and foot, under Armant de Bouchart arrived to take it over. So small a force was unable to maintain effective control, and when revolts broke out in the spring of 1192 the Templars were no doubt glad to part with the island to Guy de Lusignan. The Lusignan dynasty was to rule in Cyprus for nearly 300 years, and in the fourteenth century a branch of the family also controlled Cilicia. After Hattin (1187), when little of the mainland remained in Frankish hands, a new base was much needed. This the acquisition of Cyprus conveniently supplied. When the Kingdom of Jerusalem at last fell, the base had been in operation for a hundred years. Many had found there estates and responsibilities, and the Latin occupation of the island introduced a period of civilization, wealth and prosperity, to which the Abbey of Bella Pais and the cathedrals of Nicosia and Famagusta bear impressive witness.

It was to be expected that the building fever which possessed the Latins in the Holy Land would find a new outlet in Cyprus. Circumstances however were not the same. Castellation was a royal prerogative. Consequently castles were mainly built by the crown and, with permission, by the Military Orders. Again, the

---

* Isaac Comnenos, the Byzantine ruler who opposed Richard I, was himself a usurper. He was shipped to Palestine and was for a time imprisoned at Margat in the charge of the Hospitallers.

Latins in Cyprus, who were not under constant threat of attack across a land frontier, lacked the same inducement to modernize and reconstruct the Byzantine castles, of which, as in Syria, they found a liberal provision. There was less sense of urgency and less achievement. The Lusignans added nothing in Cyprus to the art of military fortification as it had been developed in Syria. Their main achievements were in Cilicia. In Cyprus their works were simpler and less ambitious. Though their gothic ashlar is often finely jointed, the plain barrel vault is commoner in their castle chambers than the shapely ribbed vaulting that characterizes the best Latin work on the mainland. They left no great concentric castles like Krak and Margat.

Their building achievement in Cyprus, judged by any standard less exacting than that of Latin Syria and Cilicia, is none the less impressive. It remains so in spite of much later demolition. The troubles that overtook the island in the second half of the fourteenth century, prompting the Genoese and Mameluk invasions, probably destroyed relatively little earlier work, and fortification of characteristic Crusader type continued to be built into the fifteenth century. It was the Venetian occupation after 1489 that dealt harshly with the Cyprian castles and led to the wholesale destruction and replacement of Latin fortification. The growing Turkish power, and the threat of that invasion which came ultimately in 1570 and is memorable for the determined defence of Famagusta, led the Venetians, particularly after 1550, to remodel the defences of the island. They did so thoroughly. Long anticipating the works of Vauban, they adapted their castles in the style then common in Italy, making lavish use of solid earth bastions, to resist the novel artillery of the day. Their defences at Famagusta—on which Giovanni Sanmichele worked in 1558—and at Nicosia still stand, expressing a new conception of fortification unknown to the Crusaders of the Middle Ages.

As a maritime power faced with the possibility of maritime

invasion, the Venetians concentrated on the refortification of their ports. Consequently little of the earlier Latin work survives intact at Famagusta, and much of that at Kyrenia gave place to artillery defences. At Limassol the Venetians dismantled all that survived of medieval date, excepting the shell of the chapel. The latter was to become the core of the present Turkish fort. To replace the old castle a great fortress was projected on the Akrotiri peninsular nearby, but it was never executed. The disappearance of the Templar fortress at Gastria, built before 1211 and possibly the earliest wholly Frankish castle on the island, probably antedates the Venetian occupation. Only the rock-cut ditch survives beside the sea. Inland the Venetians also wholly reconstructed the fortifications of Nicosia, and there too the Lusignan work has gone. Elsewhere in the interior, preoccupied with the control of the coast, they regarded castles as a useless expense and a possible embarrassment. The major mountain castles were dismantled some considerable time before the Turkish invasion.

The Latin castles in Cyprus were of three main types. First, there were the inland castles of no great strength. These were primarily centres of administration and strongpoints from which a restive but ill-armed population could be held in check. Secondly, there were the port fortifications. As was natural on an island these were the most considerable defensive works. Finally, there were the romantic fortresses set on the crest of the mountain range in the north—St Hilarion, Buffavento, and Kantara. These served essentially as places of refuge for the royal family, and sometimes for the dissident factions that opposed them, in the course of the dynastic quarrels that so often divided the kingdom. Their natural defences were exceptional and their sites so strong that they called for no fortification comparable to that of the large castles in the Syrian hills. Happily, and in part fortuitously, Kolossi, Kyrenia and St Hilarion still exist to offer a clear picture of these three types of castle.

Kolossi was given to the Hospitallers by Hugh I of Lusignan in 1210. After 1310, when the Order moved its headquarters to Rhodes, Kolossi remained the seat of the Grand Commandery of Cyprus. This, with the revenues of over forty villages, was once the wealthiest the Knights possessed. Kolossi must thus be envisaged as the administrative centre of a large property and as typical of a class of fort not designed primarily to resist major siege operations, though offering effective defence against sporadic revolts and raids. The castle suffered at the hands of the Genoese and Mameluks in the latter half of the fourteenth century, and was rebuilt in about 1458. A decade later John Langstrother, an Englishman, was Grand Commander and apparently made further alterations. The ultimate fate of the castle typifies that of the island. In 1488 the castle and the lands of the Grand Commandery were made over to the Venetian Giorgio Cornaro and became hereditary in the Cornaro family. A year later his sister, Katherine Cornaro, the last queen of Cyprus, resigned the kingdom itself into the hands of the Venetians.

Today little remains of the fifteenth-century castle but the keep. There are, however, vestiges of an outer curtain wall, and the plan of the place must have once resembled some of the earlier and simpler Syrian castles such as Chastel Rouge (see Fig. 11, p. 43). The keep is strong. The walls are over 9 feet thick at ground level and it is composed of three vaulted storeys and a fortified roof, in all over 75 feet high. The lowest storey, probably used as a store, and containing a cistern, is a semi-basement lighted only by narrow apertures. Though it is now served by a postern immediately below the main gate of the keep this is probably of later date; no doubt once the only entry was by the trap-door in the floor above. The main entrance to the keep was several feet above ground level and was approached up a flight of steps and across a drawbridge. It was defended by machicolation at parapet level. A circular stone staircase, set in the thickness of the wall at the south-east corner, leads from the first floor up to the roof. The second floor presumably housed the Grand Commander. It contains two large barrel-vaulted rooms, each over 50 feet long, and in the internal wall which separates them are situated the fireplaces and chimneys. From the roof the main defence of the keep was conducted. It is furnished with a crenellated parapet and the merlons themselves are pierced with loopholes. Though Kolossi is neither a beautiful nor cunning fortification, the keep must have been fully adequate to awe and administer the surrounding territory.

The Latin work at Kyrenia is of a more imposing order. The Byzantines, to whom an original rectangular castle must be attributed, chose for their site the acropolis of the classical town, a small promontory on the north coast of the island, dominating the little harbour of Kyrenia and looking across the water to the Cilician hills. Here arose, by a process of reconstruction that in the main probably post-dated the fall of Acre, the most important castle on the island. For three and a half centuries it played a vital role in the internal politics of Cyprus, and was the mainstay of the Lusignans during the Genoese occupation of Famagusta (1372–1464), resisting a vigorous Genoese siege in 1374. The characteristic siege weapons of the period were employed. After attempting to take the place by assault with scaling ladders, the Genoese sent to Famagusta for an outsize mangon which hurled immense stones. The constable in charge of the castle was an engineer and the damage was successfully repaired. The Genoese then brought up wooden assault towers, one of them three storeys high, but the defenders set fire to them. The siege was raised after the constable invited some of the Genoese knights to a banquet and gave them ocular proof of the impregnability of the defences. In 1426 at the time of the Mameluk invasion, members of the royal family with the royal treasure found security in Kyrenia, and from the strength of this single castle, Charlotte, the last legitimate Lusignan queen, with her husband maintained claim to the

28   CHASTEL PÈLERIN: Cyclopean masonry. See p. 9

sovereignty of the island for three years (1460–3). After the Venetian occupation the fortifications were considerably strengthened. It was to little purpose. At the time of the Turkish invasion the governor betrayed the castle to the Pasha of Cilicia.

Latin Kyrenia was rectangular in plan, concentric on the south and west, and buttressed by four powerful towers at the corners (those on the north-west and north-east, lapped by the waves, were square and horseshoe-shaped respectively). The castle, as we have seen, was for long periods a Lusignan residence, and among the buildings ranged round the walls of the spacious courtyard—it measures 350 feet from north to south—was a royal palace that overlooked the castle entrance and the harbour on the west. This harbour and the *bourg* behind it were ringed with their own walls, of which several towers survive.

Venetian fortification has obscured much of the earlier work. The Venetians entirely rebuilt the outer west wall and, to protect the west and south of the castle, built three ponderous tower-bastions and filled with earth the space between the inner and the outer walls. Designed to resist artillery, the resulting defences, over 70 feet tall and on the south 125 feet thick, were probably the most massive stone-faced earthworks of their type ever devised. On the north and east, where the sea provided its own security and additional fortification seemed superfluous, much Latin work fortunately survives. The fine ashlar masonry speaks of Crusader building. The north curtain, with its two fighting galleries below a parapet whose merlons are pierced for fire, and the elegant horseshoe-shaped tower at the north-east, still indicate the formidable character of the Lusignan fortress.

In Cyprus it is neither the administrative castles, like Kolossi, nor the fortified ports, like Kyrenia, that have chiefly impressed subsequent generations. Imagination has seized on the mountain strongholds of Kantara, Buffavento and St Hilarion. These castle-eyries, approached by paths that wind their precipitous way

St Hilarion: From the south. See p. 114.
Kyrenia Castle: The far tower is Venetian work. See p. 113.

upward from anemones, oleanders, and fig-trees to juniper, scrub and rock, are among the most romantic fortifications in existence. Yet by reason of their inaccessibility—the north flank at St Hilarion falls almost sheer over 1,500 feet—powerful defences were largely superfluous. Nature had already done much of the masons' work.

St Hilarion has been called 'un des plus étonnants monuments de l'étonnante architecture du moyen âge'. Considered strictly as military building, the castle hardly deserves this praise. Rather, it astonishes as something that Gustave Doré might have conceived. Set dizzily on a mountain summit in a savage landscape, it is wholly improbable. The sense of improbability is heightened by the 'wrinkled sea' far below and the snows of the Taurus perceived through French Gothic tracery. Legend permeates the castle. Here St Hilarion worked miracles at a date that is still disputed, here lived the mysterious 'Queen' of whom the local peasants speak, and who was perhaps an echo of the Cyprian Aphrodite, and here the shepherd who opens a door finds himself in an enchanted garden to emerge again years later at sunrise on a dewy morning. Even the name that the Franks gave it, Dieu d'Amour, a corruption of the classical Didymos, the latter baldly descriptive of the two-pronged crest on which it stands, is improbable and evocative.

St Hilarion had strategic importance. It guarded the only easy pass from Kyrenia to Nicosia and protected the land communications of the port. During the siege of Kyrenia in 1374 the garrison inflicted serious damage on the Genoese supply columns. The elevation of the castle, whence Cilicia seems ridiculously close, made it an invaluable observation post. Like the mountain castles in Syria it formed part of an elaborate system of communication by signal. Flares at night linked it with Kyrenia and Buffavento, and through the latter with Nicosia and Kantara.

The castle was made ready for defence in about 1228 by the

regent Jean d'Ibelin, probably as a retreat for the heir apparent and his sisters, whose safety was threatened by Frederick II. In the following year the Imperialists held the castle and were in their turn besieged by the Loyalist forces. It must have been soon after that much of the Frankish rebuilding took place. The main additions of the Lusignans, either originally massively vaulted or with steep-pitched roofs, are in their competent fourteenth-century manner. In 1348 Hugh IV retired to St Hilarion to avoid the plague, as did John, Prince of Antioch, to avoid the Genoese in 1373. With his name a grim episode is associated. By the queen-mother he was falsely given to believe that his Bulgarian mercenaries were plotting his death. Summoning his servants one by one, he had them flung into the abyss. This precipitation probably occurred from the isolated tower referred to in the penultimate paragraph of this Chapter. The prince himself was murdered soon after in Nicosia.

With the coming of the Venetians, St Hilarion was slighted. It was their policy to dismantle such inaccessible inland fortification. What they left the isolation of the site has preserved. The terrain, making attack impossible on the north and west, rendered concentric fortification unnecessary. None the less, the Byzantines devised, and the Latins improved, three separate stages of defence. First, to the south, there was the large outer bailey. Though the gate was provided with a barbican and machicolation, this area was inconsiderably defended. Little was done to improve the thin crenellated walls of Byzantine rubble and the six ill-disposed circular towers. Its function was to delay temporarily an attacking force, while exposing them to fire from the upper castle. Further, massive outworks would have been labour wasted. The approaches were so abrupt that an attacking force could hardly bring up siege-towers and heavy siege weapons.

From the bailey a steeply-inclined corridor climbed to the second stage of defence. Here were grouped, round a core of

Byzantine work which included a frescoed chapel, not only their utilitarian buildings, but a curious military plaisance, an open vaulted 'belvedere'. The ingenuity with which the builders utilized each available bit of flat rock is striking. So is their use of gabled buildings. The Latins usually and sensibly employed the flat roof of the East, but the exposure of St Hilarion at well over 2,000 feet meant that heavy snowfalls occurred in winter. These called for pitched roofs.

The third stage of defence lies to the west of the second and is reached by a further steep climb. On the north, south and west, the escarpments preclude serious attack. Cradled between the two culminating rocky crests of the mountain, the area is closed on the east or entrance side by fortification and on the west by a range of buildings that contained the Great Chamber. This elaborate and imposing structure, its doors and windows dressed with fine ashlar masonry, indicates that the third ward was in fact a *cour d'honneur* and that here was both a palace and a castle. The generous windows of the Great Chamber contained fourteenth-century tracery and in their embrasures were window seats whence the Lusignans looked down the coast to Lapithos with its vineyards and the promontory of Kormakiti.

In spite of the natural defences to the south of the *cour d'honneur*, a rock-cut stair here led to a sinuous curtain wall that followed the flow of the escarpment. Somewhat below the eastern extremity of this aery curtain, and isolated from it, stood a rectangular redoubt of massive vaulted construction. This, in extremity, may possibly have been conceived as a fourth and final line of defence to which a beleaguered garrison might retire. It is unlikely to have been used in such an extremity. The natural and contrived strength of St Hilarion, when properly manned and victualled, was such that an attacker—to whom the use of normal siege weapons was inevitably denied—could hardly have taken the second and third wards.

Though St Hilarion was fortified by nature as much as by man, the castle not unsuitably closes a survey of Crusading architecture. The isolation, the finely wrought masonry in a wild landscape, the energy that built in so inaccessible a place, its active role in a splendid and fantastic enterprise, its subsequent dereliction, and the silence that now obtains within the walls, characterize many of the great monuments of the Crusading period.

Books

The following are among the works immediately relevant to the study of Crusader castles. The authors are indebted to them in varying degrees:

CRESWELL, K. A. C., *Early Muslim Architecture*, 2 vols., Oxford, 1932 and 1940.

The Muslim Architecture of Egypt, Oxford, 1952.

'Fortification in Islam before A.D. 1250', in *Proceedings of the British Academy*, vol. XXXVIII, 1952.

DESCHAMPS, PAUL, *Le Crac des Chevaliers*, 2 vols., Paris, 1934.

La Défense du Royaume de Jérusalem, Paris, 1939.

Le Château de Saone et ses Premiers Seigneurs, Paris, 1935.

'Le Château de Saone', in the *Gazette des Beaux Arts*, December 1930.

'La Sculpture française en Palestine et en Syrie', in *Monuments et Mémoires*, vol. XXXI, 1930.

'Les Entreés des Châteaux des Croisés et leurs Défenses', in *Syria*, vol. XIII.

ENLART, CAMILLE, *Les Monuments des Croisés dans le Royaume de Jérusalem*, 2 vols., Paris, 1925.

L'Art Gothique . . . en Chypre, 2 vols., Paris, 1899.

GOUGH, M., 'Anazarbus' in *Anatolian Studies*, 1952.

JOHNS, C. N., 'Excavations at Pilgrims' Castle', in *Quarterly of the Department of Antiquities in Palestine*, vol. III, 1934.

CATHCART KING, D. J., 'The Taking of Le Crac des Chevaliers in 1271', in *Antiquity*, vol. XXIII, 1949.

LAWRENCE, T. E., *Crusader Castles*, 2 vols., Golden Cockerel Press, 1936.

LOT, FERDINAND, *L'Art Militaire et les Armées au Moyen Age*, 2 vols., Paris, 1946.

MEGAW, A. H. S., *The Castle of St Hilarion*, 4th ed., Nicosia, 1954.

OMAN, CHARLES, *A History of the Art of War in the Middle Ages*, 2 vols., 2nd ed., London, 1924. (The references to siege tactics in Chapter V of this book are in part based on Professor Oman's work.)

PALESTINE EXPLORATION FUND publications; especially *Survey of Western Palestine*, 3 vols., 1873; and *Palestine in the Crusades*, published by the Survey of Palestine, N. D. (Useful map and gazetteer.)

REY, E., *Les Monuments de l'architecture militaire des Croisés en Syrie et dans l'île de Chypre*, Paris, 1871. (Once the classic work, now superseded by Deschamps' publications.)

Les Colonies Franques de Syrie aux XII et XIII siècles, Paris, 1883.

SMAIL, R. C., 'Crusaders' Castles of the Twelfth Century' in *Cambridge Historical Journal*, vol. X, 1951.

Crusading Warfare (1097–1193), Cambridge, 1956.

There are many references to castles and to Crusading warfare both in contemporary chronicles and in modern works. The main collection of chronicles is: *Recueil des historiens des croisades*, 16 vols., Paris, 1841–1906. It contains Armenian, Greek, Arabic and Latin works. Apart from this collection, two of the most illuminating and easily available chronicles are:

The Damascus Chronicle of the Crusades, extended and translated from the Chronicle of Ibn al-Qalanisi, by H. A. R. Gibb, London, 1932.

Usamah ibn Munqidh. Memoirs edited and translated by P. K. Hitti as *An Arab-Syrian Gentleman and Warrior in the period of the Crusades*, New York, 1929.

Among modern works not specially devoted to castles and warfare the authors wish to acknowledge in particular the following:

ALISHAN, *Sissouan*. French translation, Venice, 1899.

BALDWIN, MARSHALL W. (Editor), *A History of the Crusades*, vol. I,
The First Hundred Years, Philadelphia, 1955.

BELLOC, HILAIRE, *The Crusades*, London, 1937.

CAHEN, CLAUDE, *La Syrie du Nord*, Paris, 1940.

GROUSSET, RENÉ. *Histoire des Croisades et du Royaume Franc de
Jerusalem*, 3 vols., Paris, 1934–6.

HILL, SIR GEORGE, *A History of Cyprus*, 3 vols., Cambridge, 1948.

PRAWER, J., 'Etude de quelques problèmes agraires et sociaux
d'une seigneurie croisée au XIII siècle', in *Byzantion*,
tome XXII, 1952.

RUNCIMAN, STEVEN, *A History of the Crusades*, 3 vols., Cambridge,
1951–5.

SMITH, GEORGE ADAM, *The Historical Geography of the Holy Land*,
26th ed., London, 1935.

Index

OF PLACES AND PERSONS